A.E. Housman

The Works of
A.E. Housman

with an Introduction and Bibliography

Wordsworth Poetry Library

This edition published 1994 by Wordsworth Editions Ltd,
Cumberland House, Crib Street, Ware, Hertfordshire SG12 9ET.

Copyright © Wordsworth Editions 1994.

ISBN 1-85326-411-3

Printed and bound in Denmark by Nørhaven.

The paper in this book is produced from pure wood
pulp, without the use of chlorine or any other substance
harmful to the environment. The energy used in its
production consists almost entirely of hydroelectricity
and heat generated from waste materials, thereby
conserving fossil fuels and contributing little to the
greenhouse effect.

A. E. HOUSMAN
1859-1936

THE 'Shropshire' evoked in Alfred Edward Housman's
most famous work is a half imaginary world. It is the 'land
of lost content'; a magic, somewhat hazy vision of buried
villages, thatched roofs, the talismanic charm of 'the
bluebells in the azured wood', and 'those blue remember-
ed hills'. Topographical details – Hughley, Abdon under
Clee – are by his own admission, 'sometimes quite wrong'
(letter to Maurice Pollet, 5 February 1933). Recurring
place names – Ludlow, Knighton, 'In summer time on
Bredon', 'On Wenlock Edge' – are intended to create a
region of evocative emotions, not an actual locality. For
Housman is not a pastoral poet. His countryside motif
invariably remains the background for the poems' human
subjects. Through these 'lads' – young soldiers, shepherds
and athletes – Housman can explore the helplessness of
man in an alien universe, a theme echoed by his
Cambridge contemporary, Bertrand Russell:

> 'Brief and powerless is Man's life; on him and all his race the
> slow, sure doom falls pitiless and dark. Blind to good and evil,
> reckless of destruction, omnipotent matter rolls on its relentless
> way . . .'

Though the Shropshire 'lad' was definitely an imaginative
figure, his creator admitted he had 'something of my
temper and my view of life'.

Housman's native county was in fact Worcestershire;
but the hills of Shropshire formed the western horizon of

his childhood home, and from this stemmed his sentimental attachment to the land he created in his poetry. His sensitivity to earthly beauty was heightened by the thought of human mortality, when, at the age of twelve, he was confronted with the death of his mother. In *A Shropshire Lad* XLI, natural scenes from the 'beautiful and death-struck year' offer harmonious comfort to the melancholy poet, while poems like 'The Merry Guide' (*ASL* XLII) and *Last Poems* XXXIX embody earth's loveliness in spirits or psychopompoi, who lure and enchant men's souls, laughing at mortal longings:

> And midst the fluttering legion
>   Of all that ever died
> I follow, and before us
>   Goes the delightful guide
>
> With lips that brim with laughter
>   But never once respond,
> And feet that fly on feathers,
>   And serpent-circled wand.
>
> (*A Shropshire Lad* XLII)

Housman's family belonged to a High Church branch of the Church of England ('much the best religion I have ever come across'), and the cadences of the Book of Common Prayer and the Authorised Version of the Bible were etched onto his consciousness at an early age, to reappear years later in his poems as faint and distant echoes. However, it was the discovery of *Lemprière's Classical Dictionary*, which fell into his hands at the age of eight, that converted Housman to paganism. He became, in his own words, 'a deist at thirteen and an atheist at twenty-one'. In a letter to the classical scholar Gilbert Murray, he voices a deep-rooted scepticism – 'I rather doubt if man has much to gain by substituting peace for strife, as you and Jesus Christ recommend' – which resonates as the central energy of many of his poems. In 'The Carpenter's Son' (*ASL* XLVIII), the Christ-like narrator, who 'hangs for love', implores us

> 'Comrades all, that stand and gaze,
> Walk henceforth in other ways;
> See my neck and save your own:
> Comrades all, leave ill alone.'

Similarly, in 'God's Acre' (*Additional Poems* XI),

> 'All the land's alive around
> Except the churhcyard's idle ground . . .
> This hopeless garden that they sow
> With the seeds that never grow.'

The grim cynicism of these poems, enhanced by their uncompromising heroic couplets, is typical of Housman – as typical as his dreamy evocation of 'star-filled seas' or the 'aftermaths of soft September'.

In 1870, Housman won a foundation Scholarship to Bromsgrove school, and 1877 went to St John's College, Oxford, to read classics on an annual scholarship of £100. There he formed a passionate attachment to Moses Jackson, a brilliant science student who was to be an important inspiration for his later poetry. Housman achieved a first in his Honour Moderation exams at the end of the first year, but failed his finals in Ancient History and Philosophy, and consequently left Oxford without a degree. A correspondent of the *Journal of Education* explained that Housman had chosen 'at his own discretion, to avoid the reading required . . ., and acordingly had not been classed in it.' Eleven years later, Housman justified this Cyrenaic attitude to learning:

> 'If a certain department of knowledge specially attracts a man, let him study that, and study it because it attracts him; and let

vii

Introduction

him not fabricate excuses for that which requires no excuse, but
rest assured that the reason why it most attracts him is that it is
best for him'

(*Introductory Lecture to London University*, 1892)

In 1882 he took his Civil Service exams and was
appointed as a clerk in the Patent Office in London.
Moses Jackson was also working there, and the two shared
rooms in Bayswater. Jackson married and emigrated to
India in 1887, and the loss of his friend prompted
Housman's experiments with poetry. He began writing
and re-writing in notebooks, and continued until Jackson's
death in 1923. Meanwhile, Housman Senior had fallen ill,
and Alfred signed over his share of a small legacy in order
to save his family from starvation. It was this that sealed
his determination to achieve his aim of excellence in
scholarship, and make a name for himself; remaining aloof
from his family, he spent his evenings at the British
Museum, reading extensively the Greek and Latin authors
that had been neglected during his Oxford days. His
brilliant discussion of passages in Aeschylus' *Agamemnon*,
(published in 1888), attracted much attention, and he was
appointed to the chair of Latin at London University in
1892. The Introductory Lecture he gave at London was
the only one of its kind honoured by being reprinted. Its
theme was the defence of learning for its own sake:

'Other desires perish in their gratification, but the desire of
knowledge never: the eye is not satisfied with seeing nor the ear
filled with hearing. Other desires become the occasion of pain
through the dearth of the material to gratify them, but not the
desire of knowledge: the sum of things to be known is
inexhaustible, and however long we read we shall never come to
the end of our story-book. So long as the mind of man is what it
is, it will continue to exult in advancing on the unknown
throughout the infinite field of the universe; and the tree of

Introduction

knowledge will remain for ever, as it was in the beginning, a tree to be desired to make one wise.'

In 1896, Housman offered his first collection of poems for publication. Originally entitled *Terence*, or *The Poems of Terence Hearsay*, they were rejected by Macmillan. Housman changed the title to *A Shropshire Lad*, and published the volume at his own expense. He met with little encouragement, until a reviewer for *Le Gallienne* recommended the 'exquisite simplicity' of these 63 spare verses, and another critic praised their 'heart-penetrating quality'. Public indifference gradually led to interest, and Housman's sales slowly mounted until the First World War, when *A Shropshire Lad* suddenly became immensely popular. It is not difficult to see the reasons for this popularity: Housman's themes – the passing of first love, the parting of friends, the loss of youth, unpredictable and meaningless death – must have struck a powerful emotional chord with a nation that was losing an entire generation of young men to the trenches.

Housman characteristically relates the most emotive subject matter with an unblinkingly bleak, factual tone:

> To skies that knit their heartstrings right,
> To fields that bred them brave,
> The saviours come not home to-night,
> Themselves they could not save.
>
> (*A Shropshire Lad* I)

The almost smug stylistic neatness of the final lines of this stanza intensifies their horrific irony. It is a technique deliberately reminiscent of the Scottish border ballads, in which regularity of rhythm and rhyme highlights irregularity of content. The narrative vocabulary of the ballads – brutality, murder, unjustified suffering and unrequited love – combines with a rigorous, unstintingly rhythmical swing. Housman's short, regular metres (all but 47 of his 178 published poems are in the quatrain pattern common to ballads) reproduce the uncompromisingly ruthless world of the ballads via the poetry of suggestion. Strands of the story often remain unsaid, suggested. In *The True Lover*, Housman employs the same question – answer formula of ballads like *Edward Edward* and *Earl Brand*:

> 'Oh lad, what is it, lad, that drips
>   Wet from your neck on mine?
> What is it falling on my lips,
>   My lad, that tastes of brine?
>
> Oh like enough 'tis blood, my dear,
>   For when the knife has slit
> The throat across from ear to ear
>   'Twill bleed because of it.'

(A Shropshire Lad I)

Housman was elected professor of Latin at Cambridge in 1910. He did not publish any more poetry until 1922, when *Last Poems* (41 verses lifted from his notebooks) met with great acclaim. In 1931, he published in Germany a collection of obscene passages from Latin authors, under the heading *Fraefanda*, with a learned preface of solemn irony. In 1933 he was invited to give the Leslie Stephen lecture at Cambridge. He produced for the occasion *The Name and Nature of Poetry*, in which the learned professor of Classics came charging to the defence of Romanticism, arguing that poetry should bypass thought, and plunge to the very pit of emotion. This lifelong division between classical and romantic impulses – intellect and emotion, head and heart, scholarship and poetry – has dubbed Housman 'an absolute schizophrenic', in the words of John Berryman. It has also earned him the praise of his Cambridge successor, C. O. Brink:

> 'Each activity alone – the making of pure verse and of pure scholarship – would have bought justified fame to anyone unusually gifted; their concurrence is astounding. The two gifts came out of one root . . . a quite extraordinary sensitivity and alertness allowed him to touch, as it were, the very quick of language, both in forming poetry and in doing the criticism of poetry already formed.'

FURTHER READING:

J. Bayley: *A. E. Housman's Poetry*, 1922.
C. O. Brink: *English Classical Scholarship*, 1986.
L. Housman: *A. E. Housman, A Life*, 1937.
B. J. Leggatt: *The Poetic Art of A. E. Housman*, 1978.
H. Maas (ed): *A. E. Housman: Letters*, 1971.
O. Robinson: *Angry Dust: The Poetry of A. E. Housman*, 1950.

CONTENTS

A SHROPSHIRE LAD

A Shropshire Lad

I

1887

From Clee to heaven the beacon burns,
  The shires have seen it plain,
From north and south the sign returns
  And beacons burn again.

Look left, look right, the hills are bright,
  The dales are light between,
Because 'tis fifty years to-night
  That God has saved the Queen.

Now, when the flame they watch not towers
  About the soil they trod,
Lads, we'll remember friends of ours
  Who shared the work with God.

To skies that knit their heartstrings right,
  To fields that bred them brave,
The saviours come not home to-night:
  Themselves they could not save.

It dawns in Asia, tombstones show
  And Shropshire names are read;
And the Nile spills his overflow
  Beside the Severn's dead.

A Shropshire Lad

We pledge in peace by farm and town
　The Queen they served in war,
And fire the beacons up and down
　The land they perished for.

'God save the Queen' we living sing,
　From height to height 'tis heard;
And with the rest your voices ring,
　Lads of the Fifty-third.

Oh, God will save her, fear you not:
　Be you the men you've been,
Get you the sons your fathers got,
　And God will save the Queen.

II

Loveliest of trees, the cherry now
Is hung with bloom along the bough,
And stands about the woodland ride
Wearing white for Eastertide.

Now, of my threescore years and ten,
Twenty will not come again,
And take from seventy springs a score,
It only leaves me fifty more.

And since to look at things in bloom
Fifty springs are little room,
About the woodlands I will go
To see the cherry hung with snow.

III

THE RECRUIT

Leave your home behind, lad,
    And reach your friends your hand,
And go, and luck go with you
    While Ludlow tower shall stand.

Oh, come you home of Sunday
    When Ludlow streets are still
And Ludlow bells are calling
    To farm and lane and mill,

Or come you home of Monday
    When Ludlow market hums
And Ludlow chimes are playing
    'The conquering hero comes',

Come you home a hero,
    Or come not home at all,
The lads you leave will mind you
    Till Ludlow tower shall fall.

And you will list the bugle
    That blows in lands of morn,
And make the foes of England
    Be sorry you were born.

And you till trump of doomsday
　On lands of morn may lie,
And make the hearts of comrades
　Be heavy where you die.

Leave your home behind you,
　Your friends by field and town:
Oh, town and field will mind you
　Till Ludlow tower is down.

I V

REVEILLE

Wake: the silver dusk returning
  Up the beach of darkness brims;
And the ship of sunrise burning
  Strands upon the eastern rims.

Wake: the vaulted shadow shatters,
  Trampled to the floor it spanned,
And the tent of night in tatters
  Straws the sky-pavilioned land.

Up, lad, up, 'tis late for lying:
  Hear the drums of morning play;
Hark, the empty highways crying
  'Who'll beyond the hills away?'

Towns and countries woo together,
  Forelands beacon, belfries call;
Never lad that trod on leather
  Lived to feast his heart with all.

Up, lad: thews that lie and cumber
  Sunlit pallets never thrive;
Morns abed and daylight slumber
  Were not meant for man alive.

Clay lies still, but blood's a rover;
  Breath's a ware that will not keep.
Up, lad: when the journey's over
  There'll be time enough to sleep.

V

Oh see how thick the goldcup flowers
    Are lying in field and lane,
With dandelions to tell the hours
    That never are told again.
Oh may I squire you round the meads
    And pick you posies gay?
— 'Twill do no harm to take my arm.
    'You may, young man, you may.'

Ah, spring was sent for lass and lad,
    'Tis now the blood runs gold,
And man and maid had best be glad
    Before the world is old.
What flowers to-day may flower to-morrow,
    But never as good as new.
— Suppose I wound my arm right round —
    ' ''Tis true, young man, 'tis true.'

Some lads there are, 'tis shame to say,
    That only court to thieve,
And once they bear the bloom away
    'Tis little enough they leave.
Then keep your heart for men like me
    And safe from trustless chaps.
My love is true and all for you.
    'Perhaps, young man, perhaps.'

Oh, look in my eyes then, can you doubt?
  — Why, 'tis a mile from town.
How green the grass is all about!
  We might as well sit down.
— Ah, life, what is it but a flower?
  Why must true lovers sigh?
Be kind, have pity, my own, my pretty, —
  'Good-bye, young man, good-bye.'

V I

When the lad for longing sighs,
   Mute and dull of cheer and pale,
If at death's own door he lies,
   Maiden, you can heal his ail.

Lovers' ills are all to buy:
   The wan look, the hollow tone,
The hung head, the sunken eye,
   You can have them for your own.

Buy them, buy them: eve and morn
   Lovers' ills are all to sell.
Then you can lie down forlorn;
   But the lover will be well.

VII

When smoke stood up from Ludlow,
   And mist blew off from Teme,
And blithe afield to ploughing
   Against the morning beam
   I strode beside my team,

The blackbird in the coppice
   Looked out to see me stride,
And hearkened as I whistled
   The trampling team beside,
   And fluted and replied:

'Lie down, lie down, young yeoman;
   What use to rise and rise?
Rise man a thousand mornings
   Yet down at last he lies,
   And then the man is wise.'

I heard the tune he sang me,
   And spied his yellow bill;
I picked a stone and aimed it
   And threw it with a will:
   Then the bird was still.

Then my soul within me
   Took up the blackbird's strain,
And still beside the horses
   Along the dewy lane
   It sang the song again:

'Lie down, lie down, young yeoman;
  The sun moves always west;
The road one treads to labour
  Will lead one home to rest,
  And that will be the best.'

VIII

'Farewell to barn and stack and tree,
　Farewell to Severn shore.
Terence, look your last at me,
　For I come home no more.

'The sun burns on the half-mown hill,
　By now the blood is dried;
And Maurice amongst the hay lies still
　And my knife is in his side.

'My mother thinks us long away;
　'Tis time the field were mown.
She had two sons at rising day,
　To-night she'll be alone.

'And here's a bloody hand to shake,
　And oh, man, here's good-bye;
We'll sweat no more on scythe and rake,
　My bloody hands and I.

'I wish you strength to bring you pride,
　And a love to keep you clean,
And I wish you luck, come Lammastide,
　At racing on the green.

'Long for me the rick will wait,
　And long will wait the fold,
And long will stand the empty plate,
　And dinner will be cold.'

A Shropshire Lad

IX

On moonlit heath and lonesome bank
  The sheep beside me graze;
And yon the gallows used to clank
  Fast by the four cross ways.

A careless shepherd once would keep
  The flocks by moonlight there,[1]
And high amongst the glimmering sheep
  The dead man stood on air.

They hang us now in Shrewsbury jail:
  The whistles blow forlorn,
And trains all night groan on the rail
  To men that die at morn.

There sleeps in Shrewsbury jail to-night,
  Or wakes, as may betide,
A better lad, if things went right,
  Than most that sleep outside.

And naked to the hangman's noose
  The morning clocks will ring
A neck God made for other use
  Than strangling in a string.

And sharp the link of life will snap,
  And dead on air will stand
Heels that held up as straight a chap
  As treads upon the land.

[1] Hanging in chains was called keeping sheep by moonlight.

So here I'll watch the night and wait
    To see the morning shine,
When he will hear the stroke of eight
    And not the stroke of nine;

And wish my friend as sound a sleep
    As lads' I did not know,
That shepherded the moonlit sheep
    A hundred years ago.

X

MARCH

The Sun at noon to higher air,
Unharnessing the silver Pair
That late before his chariot swam,
Rides on the gold wool of the Ram.

So braver notes the storm-cock sings
To start the rusted wheel of things,
And brutes in field and brutes in pen
Leap that the world goes round again.

The boys are up the woods with day
To fetch the daffodils away,
And home at noonday from the hills
They bring no dearth of daffodils.

Afield for palms the girls repair,
And sure enough the palms are there,
And each will find by hedge or pond
Her waving silver-tufted wand.

In farm and field through all the shire
The eye beholds the heart's desire;
Ah, let not only mine be vain,
For lovers should be loved again.

XI

On your midnight pallet lying,
    Listen, and undo the door:
Lads that waste the light in sighing
    In the dark should sigh no more;
Night should ease a lover's sorrow;
Therefore, since I go to-morrow,
    Pity me before.

In the land to which I travel,
    The far dwelling, let me say –
Once, if here the couch is gravel,
    In a kinder bed I lay,
And the breast the darnel smothers
Rested once upon another's
    When it was not clay.

XII

When I watch the living meet,
  And the moving pageant file
Warm and breathing through the street
  Where I lodge a little while,

If the heats of hate and lust
  In the house of flesh are strong,
Let me mind the house of dust
  Where my sojourn shall be long.

In the nation that is not
  Nothing stands that stood before;
There revenges are forgot,
  And the hater hates no more;

Lovers lying two and two
  Ask not whom they sleep beside,
And the bridegroom all night through
  Never turns him to the bride.

XIII

When I was one-and-twenty
  I heard a wise man say,
'Give crowns and pounds and guineas
  But not your heart away;
Give pearls away and rubies
  But keep your fancy free.'
But I was one-and-twenty,
  No use to talk to me.

When I was one-and-twenty
  I heard him say again,
'The heart out of the bosom
  Was never given in vain;
'Tis paid with sighs a plenty
  And sold for endless rue.'
And I am two-and-twenty,
  And oh, 'tis true, 'tis true.

XIV

There pass the careless people
  That call their souls their own:
Here by the road I loiter,
  How idle and alone.

Ah, past the plunge of plummet,
  In seas I cannot sound,
My heart and soul and senses,
  World without end, are drowned.

His folly has not fellow
  Beneath the blue of day
That gives to man or woman
  His heart and soul away.

There flowers no balm to sain him
  From east of earth to west
That's lost for everlasting
  The heart out of his breast.

Here by the labouring highway
  With empty hands I stroll:
Sea-deep, till doomsday morning,
  Lie lost my heart and soul.

X V

Look not in my eyes, for fear
    They mirror true the sight I see,
And there you find your face too clear
    And love it and be lost like me.
One the long nights through must lie
    Spent in star-defeated sighs,
But why should you as well as I
    Perish? gaze not in my eyes.

A Grecian lad, as I hear tell,
    One that many loved in vain,
Looked into a forest well
    And never looked away again.
There, when the turf in springtime flowers,
    With downward eye and gazes sad,
Stands amid the glancing showers
    A jonquil, not a Grecian lad.

XVI

It nods and curtseys and recovers
　　When the wind blows above,
The nettle on the graves of lovers
　　That hanged themselves for love.

The nettle nods, the wind blows over,
　　The man, he does not move,
The lover of the grave, the lover
　　That hanged himself for love.

XVII

Twice a week the winter thorough
    Here stood I to keep the goal:
Football then was fighting sorrow
    For the young man's soul.

Now in Maytime to the wicket
    Out I march with bat and pad:
See the son of grief at cricket
    Trying to be glad.

Try I will; no harm in trying:
    Wonder 'tis how little mirth
Keeps the bones of man from lying
    On the bed of earth.

XVIII

Oh, when I was in love with you,
  Then I was clean and brave,
And miles around the wonder grew
  How well did I behave.

And now the fancy passes by,
  And nothing will remain,
And miles around they'll say that I
  Am quite myself again.

XIX

TO AN ATHLETE DYING YOUNG

The time you won your town the race
We chaired you through the market-place;
Man and boy stood cheering by,
And home we brought you shoulder-high.

To-day, the road all runners come,
Shoulder-high we bring you home,
And set you at your threshold down,
Townsman of a stiller town.

Smart lad, to slip betimes away
From fields where glory does not stay
And early though the laurel grows
It withers quicker than the rose.

Eyes the shady night has shut
Cannot see the record cut,
And silence sounds no worse than cheers
After earth has stopped the ears:

Now you will not swell the rout
Of lads that wore their honours out,
Runners whom renown outran
And the name died before the man.

So set, before its echoes fade,
The fleet foot on the sill of shade,
And hold to the low lintel up
The still-defended challenge-cup.

And round that early-laurelled head
Will flock to gaze the strengthless dead,
And find unwithered on its curls
The garland briefer than a girl's.

X X

Oh fair enough are sky and plain,
  But I know fairer far:
Those are as beautiful again
  That in the water are;

The pools and rivers wash so clean
  The trees and clouds and air,
The like on earth was never seen,
  And oh that I were there.

These are the thoughts I often think
  As I stand gazing down
In act upon the cressy brink
  To strip and dive and drown;

But in the golden-sanded brooks
  And azure meres I spy
A silly lad that longs and looks
  And wishes he were I.

XXI

BREDON [1] HILL

In summertime on Bredon
　The bells they sound so clear;
Round both the shires they ring them
　In steeples far and near,
　A happy noise to hear.

Here of a Sunday morning
　My love and I would lie,
And see the coloured counties,
　And hear the larks so high
　About us in the sky.

The bells would ring to call her
　In valleys miles away:
'Come all to church, good people;
　Good people, come and pray.'
　But here my love would stay.

And I would turn and answer
　Among the springing thyme,
'Oh, peal upon our wedding,
　And we will hear the chime,
　And come to church in time.'

[1] Pronounced Breedon.

35

But when the snows at Christmas
  On Bredon top were strown,
My love rose up so early
  And stole out unbeknown
  And went to church alone.

They tolled the one bell only,
  Groom there was none to see,
The mourners followed after,
  And so to church went she,
  And would not wait for me.

The bells they sound on Bredon,
  And still the steeples hum.
'Come all to church, good people,' –
  Oh, noisy bells, be dumb;
  I hear you, I will come.

XXII

The street sounds to the soldiers' tread,
    And out we troop to see:
A single redcoat turns his head,
    He turns and looks at me.

My man, from sky to sky's so far,
    We never crossed before;
Such leagues apart the world's ends are,
    We're like to meet no more;

What thoughts at heart have you and I
    We cannot stop to tell;
But dead or living, drunk or dry,
    Soldier, I wish you well.

XXIII

The lads in their hundreds to Ludlow come in for the fair,
  There's men from the barn and the forge and the
    mill and the fold,
The lads for the girls and the lads for the liquor are there,
  And there with the rest are the lads that will never be
    old.

There's chaps from the town and the field and the till and
    the cart,
  And many to count are the stalwart, and many the
    brave,
And many the handsome of face and the handsome of
    heart,
  And few that will carry their looks or their truth to the
    grave.

I wish one could know them, I wish there were tokens to
    tell
  The fortunate fellows that now you can never discern;
And then one could talk with them friendly and wish
    them farewell
  And watch them depart on the way that they will not
    return.

But now you may stare as you like and there's nothing to
    scan;
  And brushing your elbow unguessed-at and not to be
    told
They carry back bright to the coiner the mintage of man,
  The lads that will die in their glory and never be old.

XXIV

Say, lad, have you things to do?
  Quick then, while your day's at prime.
Quick, and if 'tis work for two,
  Here am I, man: now's your time.

Send me now, and I shall go;
  Call me, I shall hear you call;
Use me ere they lay me low
  Where a man's no use at all;

Ere the wholesome flesh decay,
  And the willing nerve be numb,
And the lips lack breath to say,
  'No, my lad, I cannot come.'

XXV

This time of year a twelvemonth past,
   When Fred and I would meet,
We needs must jangle, till at last
   We fought and I was beat.

So then the summer fields about,
   Till rainy days began,
Rose Harland on her Sundays out
   Walked with the better man.

The better man she walks with still,
   Though now 'tis not with Fred:
A lad that lives and has his will
   Is worth a dozen dead.

Fred keeps the house all kinds of weather,
   And clay's the house he keeps;
When Rose and I walk out together
   Stock-still lies Fred and sleeps.

XXVI

Along the field as we came by
A year ago, my love and I,
The aspen over stile and stone
Was talking to itself alone.
'Oh who are these that kiss and pass?
A country lover and his lass;
Two lovers looking to be wed;
And time shall put them both to bed,
But she shall lie w'th earth above,
And he beside another love.'

And sure enough beneath the tree
There walks another love with me,
And overhead the aspen heaves
Its rainy-sounding silver leaves;
And I spell nothing in their stir,
But now perhaps they speak to her,
And plain for her to understand
They talk about a time at hand
When I shall sleep with clover clad,
And she beside another lad.

XXVII

'Is my team ploughing,
　　That I was used to drive
And hear the harness jingle
　　When I was man alive?'

Ay, the horses trample,
　　The harness jingles now;
No change though you lie under
　　The land you used to plough.

'Is football playing
　　Along the river shore,
With lads to chase the leather,
　　Now I stand up no more?'

Ay, the ball is flying,
　　The lads play heart and soul;
The goal stands up, the keeper
　　Stands up to keep the goal.

'Is my girl happy,
　　That I thought hard to leave,
And has she tired of weeping
　　As she lies down at eve?'

Ay, she lies down lightly,
　　She lies not down to weep:
Your girl is well contented.
　　Be still, my lad, and sleep.

'Is my friend hearty,
  Now I am thin and pine,
And has he found to sleep in
  A better bed than mine?'

Yes, lad, I lie easy,
  I lie as lads would choose;
I cheer a dead man's sweetheart,
  Never ask me whose.

XXVIII

THE WELSH MARCHES

High the vanes of Shrewsbury gleam
Islanded in Severn stream;
The bridges from the steepled crest
Cross the water east and west.

The flag of morn in conqueror's state
Enters at the English gate:
The vanquished eve, as night prevails,
Bleeds upon the road to Wales.

Ages since the vanquished bled
Round my mother's marriage-bed;
There the ravens feasted far
About the open house of war:

When Severn down to Buildwas ran
Coloured with the death of man,
Couched upon her brother's grave
The Saxon got me on the slave.

The sound of fight is silent long
That began the ancient wrong;
Long the voice of tears is still
That wept of old the endless ill.

In my heart it has not died,
The war that sleeps on Severn side;
They cease not fighting, east and west,
On the marches of my breast.

Here the truceless armies yet
Trample, rolled in blood and sweat;
They kill and kill and never die;
And I think that each is I.

None will part us, none undo
The knot that makes one flesh of two,
Sick with hatred, sick with pain,
Strangling — When shall we be slain?

When shall I be dead and rid
Of the wrong my father did?
How long, how long, till spade and hearse
Put to sleep my mother's curse?

XXIX

THE LENT LILY

'Tis spring; come out to ramble
The hilly brakes around,
For under thorn and bramble
About the hollow ground
The primroses are found.

And there's the windflower chilly
With all the winds at play,
And there's the Lenten lily
That has not long to stay
And dies on Easter day.

And since till girls go maying
You find the primrose still,
And find the windflower playing
With every wind at will,
But not the daffodil,

Bring baskets now, and sally
Upon the spring's array,
And bear from hill and valley
The daffodil away
That dies on Easter day.

X X X

Others, I am not the first,
Have willed more mischief than they durst:
If in the breathless night I too
Shiver now, 'tis nothing new.

More than I, if truth were told,
Have stood and sweated hot and cold,
And through their reins in ice and fire
Fear contended with desire.

Agued once like me were they,
But I like them shall win my way
Lastly to the bed of mould
Where there's neither heat nor cold.

But from my grave across my brow
Plays no wind of healing now,
And fire and ice within me fight
Beneath the suffocating night.

XXXI

On Wenlock Edge the wood's in trouble;
    His forest fleece the Wrekin heaves;
The gale, it plies the saplings double,
    And thick on Severn snow the leaves.

'Twould blow like this through holt and hanger
    When Uricon the city stood:
'Tis the old wind in the old anger,
    But then it threshed another wood.

Then, 'twas before my time, the Roman
    At yonder heaving hill would stare:
The blood that warms an English yeoman,
    The thoughts that hurt him, they were there.

There, like the wind through woods in riot,
    Through him the gale of life blew high;
The tree of man was never quiet:
    Then 'twas the Roman, now 'tis I.

The gale, it plies the saplings double,
    It blows so hard, 'twill soon be gone:
To-day the Roman and his trouble
    Are ashes under Uricon.

A Shropshire Lad

XXXII

From far, from eve and morning
  And yon twelve-winded sky,
The stuff of life to knit me
  Blew hither: here am I.

Now – for a breath I tarry
  Nor yet disperse apart –
Take my hand quick and tell me,
  What have you in your heart.

Speak now, and I will answer;
  How shall I help you, say;
Ere to the wind's twelve quarters
  I take my endless way.

XXXIII

If truth in hearts that perish
  Could move the powers on high,
I think the love I bear you
  Should make you not to die.

Sure, sure, if stedfast meaning,
  If single thought could save,
The world might end to-morrow,
  You should not see the grave.

This long and sure-set liking,
  This boundless will to please,
– Oh, you should live for ever
  If there were help in these.

But now, since all is idle,
  To this lost heart be kind,
Ere to a town you journey
  Where friends are ill to find.

XXXIV

THE NEW MISTRESS

'Oh, sick I am to see you, will you never let me be?
You may be good for something but you are not good for
  me.
Oh, go where you are wanted, for you are not wanted here.
And that was all the farewell when I parted from my
  dear.

'I will go where I am wanted, to a lady born and bred
Who will dress me free for nothing in a uniform of red;
She will not be sick to see me if I only keep it clean:
I will go where I am wanted for a soldier of the Queen.

'I will go where I am wanted, for the sergeant does not
  mind;
He may be sick to see me but he treats me very kind:
He gives me beer and breakfast and a ribbon for my cap,
And I never knew a sweetheart spend her money on a
  chap.

'I will go where I am wanted, where there's room for one
  or two,
And the men are none too many for the work there is to
  do;
Where the standing line wears thinner and the dropping
  dead lie thick;
And the enemies of England they shall see me and be
  sick.'

X X X V

On the idle hill of summer,
  Sleepy with the flow of streams,
Far I hear the steady drummer
  Drumming like a noise in dreams.

Far and near and low and louder
  On the roads of earth go by,
Dear to friends and food for powder,
  Soldiers marching, all to die.

East and west on fields forgotten
  Bleach the bones of comrades slain,
Lovely lads and dead and rotten;
  None that go return again.

Far the calling bugles hollo,
  High the screaming fife replies,
Gay the files of scarlet follow:
  Woman bore me, I will rise.

XXXVI

White in the moon the long road lies,
  The moon stands blank above;
White in the moon the long road lies
  That leads me from my love.

Still hangs the hedge without a gust,
  Still, still the shadows stay:
My feet upon the moonlit dust
  Pursue the ceaseless way.

The world is round, so travellers tell,
  And straight though reach the track,
Trudge on, trudge on, 'twill all be well,
  The way will guide one back.

But ere the circle homeward hies
  Far, far must it remove:
White in the moon the long road lies
  That leads me from my love.

XXXVII

As through the wild green hills of Wyre
The train ran, changing sky and shire,
And far behind, a fading crest,
Low in the forsaken west
Sank the high-reared head of Clee,
My hand lay empty on my knee.
Aching on my knee it lay:
That morning half a shire away
So many an honest fellow's fist
Had well-nigh wrung it from the wrist.
Hand, said I, since now we part
From fields and men we know by heart,
For strangers' faces, strangers' lands, –
Hand, you have held true fellows' hands.
Be clean then; rot before you do
A thing they'd not believe of you.
You and I must keep from shame
In London streets the Shropshire name;
On banks of Thames they must not say
Severn breeds worse men than they;
And friends abroad must bear in mind
Friends at home they leave behind.
Oh, I shall be stiff and cold
When I forget you, hearts of gold;
The land where I shall mind you not
Is the land where all's forgot.
And if my foot returns no more
To Teme nor Corve nor Severn shore,

A Shropshire Lad

Luck, my lads, be with you still
By falling stream and standing hill,
By chiming tower and whispering tree,
Men that made a man of me.
About your work in town and farm
Still you'll keep my head from harm,
Still you'll help me, hands that gave
A grasp to friend me to the grave.

XXXVIII

The winds out of the west land blow,
  My friends have breathed them there;
Warm with the blood of lads I know
  Comes east the sighing air.

It fanned their temples, filled their lungs,
  Scattered their forelocks free;
My friends made words of it with tongues
  That talk no more to me.

Their voices, dying as they fly,
  Loose on the wind are sown;
The names of men blow soundless by,
  My fellows' and my own.

Oh lads, at home I heard you plain,
  But here your speech is still,
And down the sighing wind in vain
  You hollo from the hill.

The wind and I, we both were there,
  But neither long abode;
Now through the friendless world we fare
  And sigh upon the road.

XXXIX

'Tis time, I think, by Wenlock town
   The golden broom should blow;
The hawthorn sprinkled up and down
   Should charge the land with snow.

Spring will not wait the loiterer's time
   Who keeps so long away;
So others wear the broom and climb
   The hedgerows heaped with may.

Oh tarnish late on Wenlock Edge,
   Gold that I never see;
Lie long, high snowdrifts in the hedge
   That will not shower on me.

A Shropshire Lad

X L

Into my heart an air that kills
From yon far country blows:
What are those blue remembered hills,
What spires, what farms are those?

That is the land of lost content,
I see it shining plain,
The happy highways where I went
And cannot come again.

XLI

In my own shire, if I was sad,
Homely comforters I had:
The earth, because my heart was sore,
Sorrowed for the son she bore;
And standing hills, long to remain,
Shared their short-lived comrade's pain.
And bound for the same bourn as I,
On every road I wandered by,
Trod beside me, close and dear,
The beautiful and death-struck year:
Whether in the woodland brown
I heard the beechnut rustle down,
And saw the purple crocus pale
Flower about the autumn dale;
Or littering far the fields of May
Lady-smocks a-bleaching lay,
And like a skylit water stood
The bluebells in the azured wood.

Yonder, lightening other loads,
The seasons range the country roads,
But here in London streets I ken
No such helpmates, only men;
And these are not in plight to bear,
If they would, another's care.
They have enough as 'tis: I see
In many an eye that measures me

The mortal sickness of a mind
Too unhappy to be kind.
Undone with misery, all they can
Is to hate their fellow man;
And till they drop they needs must still
Look at you and wish you ill.

A Shropshire Lad

XLII

THE MERRY GUIDE

Once in the wind of morning
    I ranged the thymy wold;
The world-wide air was azure
    And all the brooks ran gold.

There through the dews beside me
    Behold a youth that trod,
With feathered cap on forehead,
    And poised a golden rod.

With mien to match the morning
    And gay delightful guise
And friendly brows and laughter
    He looked me in the eyes.

Oh whence, I asked, and whither?
    He smiled and would not say,
And looked at me and beckoned
    And laughed and led the way.

And with kind looks and laughter
    And nought to say beside
We two went on together,
    I and my happy guide.

Across the glittering pastures
  And empty upland still
And solitude of shepherds
  High in the folded hill,

By hanging woods and hamlets
  That gaze through orchards down
On many a windmill turning
  And far-discovered town,

With gay regards of promise
  And sure unslackened stride
And smiles and nothing spoken
  Led on my merry guide.

By blowing realms of woodland
  With sunstruck vanes afield
And cloud-led shadows sailing
  About the windy weald,

By valley-guarded granges
  And silver waters wide,
Content at heart I followed
  With my delightful guide.

And like the cloudy shadows
  Across the country blown
We two fare on for ever,
  But not we two alone.

With the great gale we journey
   That breathes from gardens thinned,
Borne in the drift of blossoms
   Whose petals throng the wind;

Buoyed on the heaven-heard whisper
   Of dancing leaflets whirled
From all the woods that autumn
   Bereaves in all the world.

And midst the fluttering legion
   Of all that ever died
I follow, and before us
   Goes the delightful guide,

With lips that brim with laughter
   But never once respond,
And feet that fly on feathers,
   And serpent-circled wand.

XLIII

THE IMMORTAL PART

When I meet the morning beam
Or lay me down at night to dream,
I hear my bones within me say,
'Another night, another day.

'When shall this slough of sense be cast,
This dust of thoughts be laid at last,
The man of flesh and soul be slain
And the man of bone remain?

'This tongue that talks, these lungs that shout,
These thews that hustle us about,
This brain that fills the skull with schemes,
And its humming hive of dreams,—

'These to-day are proud in power
And lord it in their little hour:
The immortal bones obey control
Of dying flesh and dying soul.

' 'Tis long till eve and morn are gone:
Slow the endless night comes on,
And late to fulness grows the birth
That shall last as long as earth.

'Wanderers eastward, wanderers west,
Know you why you cannot rest?
'Tis that every mother's son
Travails with a skeleton.

'Lie down in the bed of dust;
Bear the fruit that bear you must;
Bring the eternal seed to light,
And morn is all the same as night.

'Rest you so from trouble sore,
Fear the heat o' the sun no more,
Nor the snowing winter wild,
Now you labour not with child.

'Empty vessel, garment cast,
We that wore you long shall last.
– Another night, another day.'
So my bones within me say.

Therefore they shall do my will
To-day while I am master still,
And flesh and soul, now both are strong,
Shall hale the sullen slaves along,

Before this fire of sense decay,
This smoke of thought blow clean away,
And leave with ancient night alone
The stedfast and enduring bone.

XLIV

Shot? so quick, so clean an ending?
  Oh that was right, lad, that was brave:
Yours was not an ill for mending,
  'Twas best to take it to the grave.

Oh you had forethought, you could reason,
  And saw your road and where it led,
And early wise and brave in season
  Put the pistol to your head.

Oh soon, and better so than later
  After long disgrace and scorn,
You shot dead the household traitor,
  The soul that should not have been born.

Right you guessed the rising morrow
  And scorned to tread the mire you must:
Dust's your wages, son of sorrow,
  But men may come to worse than dust.

Souls undone, undoing others, —
  Long time since the tale began.
You would not live to wrong your brothers:
  Oh lad, you died as fits a man.

Now to your grave shall friend and stranger
  With ruth and some with envy come:
Undishonoured, clear of danger,
  Clean of guilt, pass hence and home.

Turn safe to rest, no dreams, no waking;
   And here, man, here's the wreath I've made:
'Tis not a gift that's worth the taking,
   But wear it and it will not fade.

A Shropshire Lad

XLV

If it chance your eye offend you,
  Pluck it out, lad, and be sound:
'Twill hurt, but here are salves to friend you,
  And many a balsam grows on ground.

And if your hand or foot offend you,
  Cut it off, lad, and be whole;
But play the man, stand up and end you,
  When your sickness is your soul.

X L V I

Bring, in this timeless grave to throw,
No cypress, sombre on the snow;
Snap not from the bitter yew
His leaves that live December through;
Break no rosemary, bright with rime
And sparkling to the cruel clime;
Nor plod the winter land to look
For willows in the icy brook
To cast them leafless round him: bring
No spray that ever buds in spring.

But if the Christmas field has kept
Awns the last gleaner overstept,
Or shrivelled flax, whose flower is blue
A single season, never two;
Or if one haulm whose year is o'er
Shivers on the upland frore,
– Oh, bring from hill and stream and plain
Whatever will not flower again,
To give him comfort: he and those
Shall bide eternal bedfellows
Where low upon the couch he lies
Whence he never shall arise.

XLVII

THE CARPENTER'S SON

'Here the hangman stops his cart:
Now the best of friends must part.
Fare you well, for ill fare I:
Live, lads, and I will die.

'Oh, at home had I but stayed
'Prenticed to my father's trade,
Had I stuck to plane and adze,
I had not been lost, my lads.

'Then I might have built perhaps
Gallows-trees for other chaps,
Never dangled on my own,
Had I but left ill alone.

'Now, you see, they hang me high,
And the people passing by
Stop to shake their fists and curse;
So 'tis come from ill to worse.

'Here hang I, and right and left
Two poor fellows hang for theft:
All the same's the luck we prove,
Though the midmost hangs for love.

'Comrades all, that stand and gaze,
Walk henceforth in other ways;
See my neck and save your own:
Comrades all, leave ill alone.

'Make some day a decent end,
Shrewder fellows than your friend.
Fare you well, for ill fare I:
Live, lads, and I will die.'

XLVIII

Be still, my soul, be still; the arms you bear are brittle,
  Earth and high heaven are fixt of old and founded
    strong.
Think rather, -- call to thought, if now you grieve a little,
  The days when we had rest, O soul, for they were long.

Men loved unkindness then, but lightless in the quarry
  I slept and saw not; tears fell down, I did not mourn;
Sweat ran and blood sprang out and I was never sorry:
  Then it was well with me, in days ere I was born.

Now, and I muse for why and never find the reason,
  I pace the earth, and drink the air, and feel the sun.
Be still, be still, my soul; it is but for a season:
  Let us endure an hour and see injustice done.

Ay, look: high heaven and earth ail from the prime
    foundation;
  All thoughts to rive the heart are here, and all are vain:
Horror and scorn and hate and fear and indignation --
  Oh why did I awake? when shall I sleep again?

XLIX

Think no more, lad; laugh, be jolly:
  Why should men make haste to die?
Empty heads and tongues a-talking
Make the rough road easy walking,
And the feather pate of folly
  Bears the falling sky.

Oh, 'tis jesting, dancing, drinking
  Spins the heavy world around.
If young hearts were not so clever,
Oh, they would be young for ever:
Think no more; 'tis only thinking
  Lays lads underground.

L

Clunton and Clunbury,
  Clungunford and Clun,
Are the quietest places
  Under the sun.

In valleys of springs of rivers,
  By Ony and Teme and Clun,
The country for easy livers,
  The quietest under the sun,

We still had sorrows to lighten,
  One could not be always glad,
And lads knew trouble at Knighton
  When I was a Knighton lad.

By bridges that Thames runs under,
  In London, the town built ill,
'Tis sure small matter for wonder
  If sorrow is with one still.

And if as a lad grows older
  The troubles he bears are more,
He carries his griefs on a shoulder
  That handselled them long before.

Where shall one halt to deliver
  This luggage I'd lief set down?
Not Thames, not Teme is the river,
  Nor London nor Knighton the town:

74

A Shropshire Lad

'Tis a long way further than Knighton,
A quieter place than Clun,
Where doomsday may thunder and lighten
And little 'twill matter to one.

L I

Loitering with a vacant eye
Along the Grecian gallery,
And brooding on my heavy ill,
I met a statue standing still.
Still in marble stone stood he,
And stedfastly he looked at me.
'Well met,' I thought the look would say,
'We both were fashioned far away;
We neither knew, when we were young,
These Londoners we live among.'

Still he stood and eyed me hard,
An earnest and a grave regard:
'What, lad, drooping with your lot?
I too would be where I am not.
I too survey that endless line
Of men whose thoughts are not as mine.
Years, ere you stood up from rest,
On my neck the collar prest;
Years, when you lay down your ill,
I shall stand and bear it still.
Courage, lad, 'tis not for long:
Stand, quit you like stone, be strong.'
So I thought his look would say;
And light on me my trouble lay,
And I stept out in flesh and bone
Manful like the man of stone.

L I I

Far in a western brookland
  That bred me long ago
The poplars stand and tremble
  By pools I used to know.

There, in the windless night-time,
  The wanderer, marvelling why,
Halts on the bridge to hearken
  How soft the poplars sigh.

He hears: no more remembered
  In fields where I was known,
Here I lie down in London
  And turn to rest alone.

There, by the starlit fences,
  The wanderer halts and hears
My soul that lingers sighing
  About the glimmering weirs.

LIII

THE TRUE LOVER

The lad came to the door at night,
    When lovers crown their vows,
And whistled soft and out of sight
    In shadow of the boughs.

'I shall not vex you with my face
    Henceforth, my love, for aye;
So take me in your arms a space
    Before the east is grey.

'When I from hence away am past
    I shall not find a bride,
And you shall be the first and last
    I ever lay beside.'

She heard and went and knew not why;
    Her heart to his she laid;
Light was the air beneath the sky
    But dark under the shade.

'Oh do you breathe, lad, that your breast
    Seems not to rise and fall,
And here upon my bosom prest
    There beats no heart at all?'

'Oh loud, my girl, it once would knock,
   You should have felt it then;
But since for you I stopped the clock
   It never goes again.'

'Oh lad, what is it, lad, that drips
   Wet from your neck on mine?
What is it falling on my lips,
   My lad, that tastes of brine?'

'Oh like enough 'tis blood, my dear,
   For when the knife has slit
The throat across from ear to ear
   'Twill bleed because of it.'

Under the stars the air was light
   But dark below the boughs,
The still air of the speechless night,
   When lovers crown their vows.

L I V

With rue my heart is laden
    For golden friends I had,
For many a rose-lipt maiden
    And many a lightfoot lad.

By brooks too broad for leaping
    The lightfoot boys are laid;
The rose-lipt girls are sleeping
    In fields where roses fade.

A Shropshire Lad

LV

Westward on the high-hilled plains
  Where for me the world began,
Still, I think, in newer veins
  Frets the changeless blood of man.

Now that other lads than I
  Strip to bathe on Severn shore,
They, no help, for all they try,
  Tread the mill I trod before.

There, when hueless is the west
  And the darkness hushes wide,
Where the lad lies down to rest
  Stands the troubled dream beside.

There, on thoughts that once were mine,
  Day looks down the eastern steep,
And the youth at morning shine
  Makes the vow he will not keep.

L V I

THE DAY OF BATTLE

'Far I hear the bugle blow
To call me where I would not go,
And the guns begin the song,
"Soldier, fly or stay for long."

'Comrade, if to turn and fly
Made a soldier never die,
Fly I would, for who would not?
'Tis sure no pleasure to be shot.

'But since the man that runs away
Lives to die another day,
And cowards' funerals, when they come,
Are not wept so well at home,

'Therefore, though the best is bad,
Stand and do the best, my lad;
Stand and fight and see your slain,
And take the bullet in your brain.'

LVII

You smile upon your friend to-day,
    To-day his ills are over;
You hearken to the lover's say,
    And happy is the lover.

'Tis late to hearken, late to smile,
    But better late than never:
I shall have lived a little while
    Before I die for ever.

LVIII

When I came last to Ludlow
　　Amidst the moonlight pale,
Two friends kept step beside me,
　　Two honest lads and hale.

Now Dick lies long in the churchyard,
　　And Ned lies long in jail,
And I come home to Ludlow
　　Amidst the moonlight pale.

LIX

THE ISLE OF PORTLAND

The star-filled seas are smooth to-night
   From France to England strown;
Black towers above the Portland light
   The felon-quarried stone.

On yonder island, not to rise,
   Never to stir forth free,
Far from his folk a dead lad lies
   That once was friends with me.

Lie you easy, dream you light,
   And sleep you fast for aye;
And luckier may you find the night
   Than ever you found the day.

A Shropshire Lad

LX

Now hollow fires burn out to black,
    And lights are guttering low:
Square your shoulders, lift your pack,
    And leave your friends and go.

Oh never fear, man, nought's to dread,
    Look not left nor right:
In all the endless road you tread
    There's nothing but the night.

LXI

HUGHLEY STEEPLE

The vane on Hughley steeple
  Veers bright, a far-known sign,
And there lie Hughley people,
  And there lie friends of mine.
Tall in their midst the tower
  Divides the shade and sun,
And the clock strikes the hour
  And tells the time to none.

To south the headstones cluster,
  The sunny mounds lie thick;
The dead are more in muster
  At Hughley than the quick.
North, for a soon-told number,
  Chill graves the sexton delves,
And steeple-shadowed slumber
  The slayers of themselves.

To north, to south, lie parted,
  With Hughley tower above,
The kind, the single-hearted,
  The lads I used to love.
And, south or north, 'tis only
  A choice of friends one knows,
And I shall ne'er be lonely
  Asleep with these or those.

LXII

'Terence, this is stupid stuff:
You eat your victuals fast enough;
There can't be much amiss, 'tis clear,
To see the rate you drink your beer.
But oh, good Lord, the verse you make,
It gives a chap the belly-ache.
The cow, the old cow, she is dead;
It sleeps well, the horned head:
We poor lads, 'tis our turn now
To hear such tunes as killed the cow.
Pretty friendship 'tis to rhyme
Your friends to death before their time
Moping melancholy mad:
Come, pipe a tune to dance to, lad.'

Why, if 'tis dancing you would be,
There's brisker pipes than poetry.
Say, for what were hop-yards meant,
Or why was Burton built on Trent?
Oh many a peer of England brews
Livelier liquor than the Muse,
And malt does more than Milton can
To justify God's ways to man.
Ale, man, ale's the stuff to drink
For fellows whom it hurts to think:
Look into the pewter pot
To see the world as the world's not.

And faith, 'tis pleasant till 'tis past:
The mischief is that 'twill not last.
Oh I have been to Ludlow fair
And left my necktie God knows where,
And carried half-way home, or near,
Pints and quarts of Ludlow beer:
Then the world seemed none so bad,
And I myself a sterling lad;
And down in lovely muck I've lain,
Happy till I woke again.
Then I saw the morning sky:
Heigho, the tale was all a lie;
The world, it was the old world yet,
I was I, my things were wet,
And nothing now remained to do
But begin the game anew.

Therefore, since the world has still
Much good, but much less good than ill,
And while the sun and moon endure
Luck's a chance, but trouble's sure,
I'd face it as a wise man would,
And train for ill and not for good.
'Tis true, the stuff I bring for sale
Is not so brisk a brew as ale:
Out of a stem that scored the hand
I wrung it in a weary land.
But take it: if the smack is sour,
The better for the embittered hour;

It should do good to heart and head
When your soul is in my soul's stead;
And I will friend you, if I may,
In the dark and cloudy day.

There was a king reigned in the East:
There, when kings will sit to feast,
They get their fill before they think
With poisoned meat and poisoned drink.
He gathered all that springs to birth
From the many-venomed earth;
First a little, thence to more,
He sampled all her killing store;
And easy, smiling, seasoned sound,
Sate the king when healths went round.
They put arsenic in his meat
And stared aghast to watch him eat;
They poured strychnine in his cup
And shook to see him drink it up:
They shook, they stared as white's their shirt:
Them it was their poison hurt.
– I tell the tale that I heard told.
Mithridates, he died old.

LXIII

I hoed and trenched and weeded,
    And took the flowers to fair:
I brought them home unheeded;
    The hue was not the wear.

So up and down I sow them
    For lads like me to find,
When I shall lie below them,
    A dead man out of mind.

Some seed the birds devour,
    And some the season mars,
But here and there will flower
    The solitary stars,

And fields will yearly bear them
    As light-leaved spring comes on,
And luckless lads will wear them
    When I am dead and gone.

LAST POEMS

We'll to the woods no more,
The laurels all are cut,
The bowers are bare of bay
That once the Muses wore;
The year draws in the day
And soon will evening shut:
The laurels all are cut,
We'll to the woods no more.
Oh we'll no more, no more
To the leafy woods away,
To the high wild woods of laurel
And the bowers of bay no more.

Last Poems

THE WEST

Beyond the moor and mountain crest
– Comrade, look not on the west –
The sun is down and drinks away
From air and land the lees of day.

The long cloud and the single pine
Sentinel the ending line,
And out beyond it, clear and wan,
Reach the gulfs of evening on.

The son of woman turns his brow
West from forty counties now,
And, as the edge of heaven he eyes,
Thinks eternal thoughts, and sighs.

Oh wide's the world, to rest or roam,
With change abroad and cheer at home,
Fights and furloughs, talk and tale,
Company and beef and ale.

But if I front the evening sky
Silent on the west look I,
And my comrade, stride for stride,
Paces silent at my side.

Comrade, look not on the west:
'Twill have the heart out of your breast;
'Twill take your thoughts and sink them far,
Leagues beyond the sunset bar.

Oh lad, I fear that yon's the sea
Where they fished for you and me,
And there, from whence we both were ta'en,
You and I shall drown again.

Send not on your soul before
To dive from that beguiling shore,
And let not yet the swimmer leave
His clothes upon the sands of eve.

Too fast to yonder strand forlorn
We journey, to the sunken bourn,
To flush the fading tinges eyed
By other lads at eventide.

Wide is the world, to rest or roam,
And early 'tis for turning home:
Plant your heel on earth and stand,
And let's forget our native land.

When you and I are spilt on air
Long we shall be strangers there;
Friends of flesh and bone are best:
Comrade, look not on the west.

II

As I gird on for fighting
    My sword upon my thigh,
I think on old ill fortunes
    Of better men than I.

Think I, the round world over,
    What golden lads are low
With hurts not mine to mourn for
    And shames I shall not know.

What evil luck soever
    For me remains in store,
'Tis sure much finer fellows
    Have fared much worse before.

So here are things to think on
    That ought to make me brave,
As I strap on for fighting
    My sword that will not save.

III

Her strong enchantments failing,
   Her towers of fear in wreck,
Her limbecks dried of poisons
   And the knife at her neck,

The Queen of air and darkness
   Begins to shrill and cry,
'O young man, O my slayer,
   To-morrow you shall die.'

O Queen of air and darkness,
   I think 'tis truth you say,
And I shall die to-morrow;
   But you will die to-day.

IV

ILLIC JACET

Oh hard is the bed they have made him,
  And common the blanket and cheap;
But there he will lie as they laid him:
  Where else could you trust him to sleep?

To sleep when the bugle is crying
  And cravens have heard and are brave,
When mothers and sweethearts are sighing
  And lads are in love with the grave.

Oh dark is the chamber and lonely,
  And lights and companions depart;
But lief will he lose them and only
  Behold the desire of his heart.

And low is the roof, but it covers
  A sleeper content to repose;
And far from his friends and his lovers
  He lies with the sweetheart he chose.

V

GRENADIER

The Queen she sent to look for me,
  The sergeant he did say,
'Young man, a soldier will you be
  For thirteen pence a day?'

For thirteen pence a day did I
  Take off the things I wore,
And I have marched to where I lie,
  And I shall march no more.

My mouth is dry, my shirt is wet,
  My blood runs all away,
So now I shall not die in debt
  For thirteen pence a day.

To-morrow after new young men
  The sergeant he must see,
For things will all be over then
  Between the Queen and me.

And I shall have to bate my price,
  For in the grave, they say,
Is neither knowledge nor device
  Nor thirteen pence a day.

VI

LANCER

I 'listed at home for a lancer,
  Oh who would not sleep with the brave?
I 'listed at home for a lancer
  · To ride on a horse to my grave.

And over the seas we were bidden
  A country to take and to keep;
And far with the brave I have ridden,
  And now with the brave I shall sleep.

For round me the men will be lying
  That learned me the way to behave,
And showed me my business of dying:
  Oh who would not sleep with the brave?

They ask and there is not an answer;
Says I, I will 'list for a lancer,
  Oh who would not sleep with the brave?

And I with the brave shall be sleeping
  At ease on my mattress of loam,
When back from their taking and keeping
  · The squadron is riding at home.

The wind with the plumes will be playing,
  The girls will stand watching them wave,
And eyeing my comrades and saying
    Oh who would not sleep with the brave?

They ask and there is not an answer;
Says you, I will 'list for a lancer,
    Oh who would not sleep with the brave?

VII

In valleys green and still
　Where lovers wander maying
They hear from over hill
　A music playing.

Behind the drum and fife,
　Past hawthornwood and hollow,
Through earth and out of life
　The soldiers follow.

The soldier's is the trade:
　In any wind or weather
He steals the heart of maid
　And man together.

The lover and his lass
　Beneath the hawthorn lying
Have heard the soldiers pass,
　And both are sighing.

And down the distance they
　With dying note and swelling
Walk the resounding way
　To the still dwelling.

VIII

Soldier from the wars returning,
   Spoiler of the taken town,
Here is ease that asks not earning;
   Turn you in and sit you down.

Peace is come and wars are over,
   Welcome you and welcome all,
While the charger crops the clover
   And his bridle hangs in stall.

Now no more of winters biting,
   Filth in trench from fall to spring,
Summers full of sweat and fighting
   For the Kesar or the King.

Rest you, charger, rust you, bridle;
   Kings and kesars, keep your pay;
Soldier, sit you down and idle
   At the inn of night for aye.

IX

The chestnut casts his flambeaux, and the flowers
   Stream from the hawthorn on the wind away,
The doors clap to, the pane is blind with showers.
   Pass me the can, lad; there's an end of May.

There's one spoilt spring to scant our mortal lot,
   One season ruined of our little store.
May will be fine next year as like as not:
   Oh ay, but then we shall be twenty-four.

We for a certainty are not the first
   Have sat in taverns while the tempest hurled
Their hopeful plans to emptiness, and cursed
   Whatever brute and blackguard made the world.

It is in truth iniquity on high
   To cheat our sentenced souls of aught they crave,
And mar the merriment as you and I
   Fare on our long fool's-errand to the grave.

Iniquity it is; but pass the can.
   My lad, no pair of kings our mothers bore;
Our only portion is the estate of man:
   We want the moon, but we shall get no more.

If here to-day the cloud of thunder lours
   To-morrow it will hie on far behests;
The flesh will grieve on other bones than ours
   Soon, and the soul will mourn in other breasts.

The troubles of our proud and angry dust
   Are from eternity, and shall not fail.
Bear them we can, and if we can we must.
   Shoulder the sky, my lad, and drink your ale.

X

Could man be drunk for ever
   With liquor, love, or fights,
Lief should I rouse at morning
   And lief lie down of nights.

But men at whiles are sober
   And think by fits and starts,
And if they think, they fasten
   Their hands upon their hearts.

X I

Yonder see the morning blink:
  The sun is up, and up must I,
To wash and dress and eat and drink
And look at things and talk and think
  And work, and God knows why.

Oh often have I washed and dressed
  And what's to show for all my pain?
Let me lie abed and rest:
Ten thousand times I've done my best
  And all's to do again.

XII

The laws of God, the laws of man,
He may keep that will and can;
Not I: let God and man decree
Laws for themselves and not for me;
And if my ways are not as theirs
Let them mind their own affairs.
Their deeds I judge and much condemn,
Yet when did I make laws for them?
Please yourselves, say I, and they
Need only look the other way.
But no, they will not; they must still
Wrest their neighbour to their will,
And make me dance as they desire
With jail and gallows and hell-fire.
And how am I to face the odds
Of man's bedevilment and God's?
I, a stranger and afraid
In a world I never made.
They will be master, right or wrong;
Though both are foolish, both are strong.
And since, my soul, we cannot fly
To Saturn nor to Mercury,
Keep we must, if keep we can,
These foreign laws of God and man.

XIII

THE DESERTER

'What sound awakened me, I wonder,
    For now 'tis dumb.'
'Wheels on the road most like, or thunder:
    Lie down; 'twas not the drum.'

Toil at sea and two in haven
    And trouble far:
Fly, crow, away, and follow, raven,
    And all that croaks for war.

'Hark, I heard the bugle crying,
    And where am I?
My friends are up and dressed and dying,
    And I will dress and die.'

'Oh love is rare and trouble plenty
    And carrion cheap,
And daylight dear at four-and-twenty:
    Lie down again and sleep.'

'Reach me my belt and leave your prattle:
    Your hour is gone;
But my day is the day of battle,
    And that comes dawning on.

'They mow the field of man in season:
   Farewell, my fair,
And, call it truth or call it treason,
   Farewell the vows that were.'

'Ay, false heart, forsake me lightly:
   'Tis like the brave.
They find no bed to joy in rightly
   Before they find the grave.

'Their love is for their own undoing,
   And east and west
They scour about the world a-wooing
   The bullet to their breast.

'Sail away the ocean over,
   Oh sail away,
And lie there with your leaden lover
   For ever and a day.'

XIV

THE CULPRIT

The night my father got me
  His mind was not on me;
He did not plague his fancy
  To muse if I should be
  The son you see.

The day my mother bore me
  She was a fool and glad,
For all the pain I cost her,
  That she had borne the lad
  That borne she had.

My mother and my father
  Out of the light they lie;
The warrant would not find them,
  And here 'tis only I
  Shall hang so high.

Oh let not man remember
  The soul that God forgot,
But fetch the county kerchief
  And noose me in the knot,
  And I will rot.

For so the game is ended
  That should not have begun.
My father and my mother
  They had a likely son,
  And I have none.

XV

EIGHT O'CLOCK

He stood, and heard the steeple
  Sprinkle the quarters on the morning town.
One, two, three, four, to market-place and people
  It tossed them down.

Strapped, noosed, nighing his hour,
  He stood and counted them and cursed his luck:
And then the clock collected in the tower
  Its strength, and struck.

XVI

SPRING MORNING

Star and coronal and bell
   April underfoot renews,
And the hope of man as well
   Flowers among the morning dews.

Now the old come out to look,
   Winter past and winter's pains,
How the sky in pool and brook
   Glitters on the grassy plains.

Easily the gentle air
   Wafts the turning season on;
Things to comfort them are there,
   Though 'tis true the best are gone.

Now the scorned unlucky lad
   Rousing from his pillow gnawn
Mans his heart and deep and glad
   Drinks the valiant air of dawn.

Half the night he longed to die,
   Now are sown on hill and plain
Pleasures worth his while to try
   Ere he longs to die again.

Blue the sky from east to west
   Arches, and the world is wide,
Though the girl he loves the best
   Rouses from another's side.

XVII

ASTRONOMY

The Wain upon the northern steep
   Descends and lifts away.
Oh I will sit me down and weep
   For bones in Africa.

For pay and medals, name and rank,
   Things that he has not found,
He hove the Cross to heaven and sank
   The pole-star underground.

And now he does not even see
   Signs of the nadir roll
At night over the ground where he
   Is buried with the pole.

XVIII

The rain, it streams on stone and hillock,
  The boot clings to the clay.
Since all is done that's due and right
Let's home; and now, my lad, good-night,
  For I must turn away.

Good-night, my lad, for nought's eternal;
  No league of ours, for sure.
To-morrow I shall miss you less,
And ache of heart and heaviness
  Are things that time should cure.

Over the hill the highway marches
  And what's beyond is wide:
Oh soon enough will pine to nought
Remembrance and the faithful thought
  That sits the grave beside.

The skies, they are not always raining
  Nor grey the twelvemonth through;
And I shall meet good days and mirth,
And range the lovely lands of earth
  With friends no worse than you.

But oh, my man, the house is fallen
  That none can build again;
My man, how full of joy and woe
Your mother bore you years ago
  To-night to lie in the rain.

XIX

In midnights of November,
　　When Dead Man's Fair is nigh,
And danger in the valley,
　　And anger in the sky,

Around the huddling homesteads
　　The leafless timber roars,
And the dead call the dying
　　And finger at the doors.

Oh, yonder faltering fingers
　　Are hands I used to hold;
Their false companion drowses
　　And leaves them in the cold.

Oh, to the bed of ocean,
　　To Africk and to Ind,
I will arise and follow
　　Along the rainy wind.

The night goes out and under
　　With all its train forlorn;
Hues in the east assemble
　　And cocks crow up the morn.

The living are the living
　　And dead the dead will stay,
And I will sort with comrades
　　That face the beam of day.

X X

The night is freezing fast,
   To-morrow comes December;
     And winterfalls of old
Are with me from the past;
   And chiefly I remember
     How Dick would hate the cold.

Fall, winter, fall; for he,
   Prompt hand and headpiece clever,
     Has woven a winter robe,
And made of earth and sea
   His overcoat for ever,
     And wears the turning globe.

X X I

The fairies break their dances
    And leave the printed lawn,
And up from India glances
    The silver sail of dawn.

The candles burn their sockets,
    The blinds let through the day,
The young man feels his pockets
    And wonders what's to pay.

X X I I

The sloe was lost in flower,
    The April elm was dim;
That was the lover's hour,
    The hour for lies and him.

If thorns are all the bower,
    If north winds freeze the fir,
Why, 'tis another's hour,
    The hour for truth and her.

XXIII

In the morning, in the morning,
  In the happy field of hay,
Oh they looked at one another
  By the light of day.

In the blue and silver morning
  On the haycock as they lay,
Oh they looked at one another
  And they looked away.

XXIV

EPITHALAMIUM

He is here, Urania's son,
Hymen come from Helicon;
God that glads the lover's heart,
He is here to join and part,
So the groomsman quits your side
And the bridegroom seeks the bride:
Friend and comrade yield you o'er
To her that hardly loves you more.

Now the sun his skyward beam
Has tilted from the Ocean stream.
Light the Indies, laggard sun:
Happy bridegroom, day is done,
And the star from Œta's steep
Calls to bed but not to sleep.

Happy bridegroom, Hesper brings
All desired and timely things.
All whom morning sends to roam,
Hesper loves to lead them home.
Home return who him behold,
Child to mother, sheep to fold,
Bird to nest from wandering wide:
Happy bridegroom, seek your bride.

Pour it out, the golden cup
Given and guarded, brimming up,
Safe through jostling markets borne
And the thicket of the thorn;
Folly spurned and danger past,
Pour it to the god at last.

Now, to smother noise and light,
Is stolen abroad the wildering night,
And the blotting shades confuse
Path and meadow full of dews;
And the high heavens, that all control,
Turn in silence round the pole.
Catch the starry beams they shed
Prospering the marriage bed,
And breed the land that reared your prime
Sons to stay the rot of time.
All is quiet, no alarms;
Nothing fear of nightly harms.
Safe you sleep on guarded ground,
And in silent circle round
The thoughts of friends keep watch and ward,
Harnessed angels, hand on sword.

XXV

THE ORACLES

'Tis mute, the word they went to hear on high Dodona
    mountain
    When winds were in the oakenshaws and all the caul-
        drons tolled,
And mute's the midland navel-stone beside the singing
    fountain,
    And echoes list to silence now where gods told lies of
        old.

I took my question to the shrine that has not ceased from
    speaking,
    The heart within, that tells the truth and tells it twice
        as plain;
And from the cave of oracles I heard the priestess shrieking
    That she and I should surely die and never live again.

Oh priestess, what you cry is clear, and sound good sense
    I think it;
    But let the screaming echoes rest, and froth your
        mouth no more.
'Tis true there's better boose than brine, but he that
    drowns must drink it;
    And oh, my lass, the news is news that men have heard
        before.

Last Poems

*The King with half the East at heel is marched from lands
   of morning;*
   *Their fighters drink the rivers up, their shafts benight
   the air.*
*And he that stands will die for nought, and home there's
   no returning.*
   The Spartans on the sea-wet rock sat down and combed
   their hair.

XXVI

The half-moon westers low, my love,
   And the wind brings up the rain;
And wide apart lie we, my love,
   And seas between the twain.

I know not if it rains, my love,
   In the land where you do lie;
And oh, so sound you sleep, my love,
   You know no more than I.

XXVII

The sigh that heaves the grasses
  Whence thou wilt never rise
Is of the air that passes
  And knows not if it sighs.

The diamond tears adorning
  Thy low mound on the lea,
Those are the tears of morning,
  That weeps, but not for thee.

XXVIII

Now dreary dawns the eastern light,
  And fall of eve is drear,
And cold the poor man lies at night,
  And so goes out the year.

Little is the luck I've had,
  And oh, 'tis comfort small
To think that many another lad
  Has had no luck at all.

XXIX

Wake not for the world-heard thunder
   Nor the chime that earthquakes toll.
Star may plot in heaven with planet,
Lightning rive the rock of granite,
Tempest tread the oakwood under:
   Fear not you for flesh nor soul.
Marching, fighting, victory past,
Stretch your limbs in peace at last.

Stir not for the soldiers drilling
   Nor the fever nothing cures:
Throb of drum and timbal's rattle
Call but man alive to battle,
And the fife with death-notes filling
   Screams for blood but not for yours.
Times enough you bled your best;
Sleep on now, and take your rest.

Sleep, my lad; the French are landed,
   London's burning, Windsor's down;
Clasp your cloak of earth about you,
We must man the ditch without you,
March unled and fight short-handed,
   Charge to fall and swim to drown.
Duty, friendship, bravery o'er,
Sleep away, lad; wake no more.

XXX

SINNER'S RUE

I walked alone and thinking,
   And faint the nightwind blew
And stirred on mounds at crossways
   The flower of sinner's rue.

Where the roads part they bury
   Him that his own hand slays,
And so the weed of sorrow
   Springs at the four cross ways.

By night I plucked it hueless,
   When morning broke 'twas blue:
Blue at my breast I fastened
   The flower of sinner's rue.

It seemed a herb of healing,
   A balsam and a sign,
Flower of a heart whose trouble
   Must have been worse than mine.

Dead clay that did me kindness,
   I can do none to you,
But only wear for breastknot
   The flower of sinner's rue.

XXXI

HELL GATE

Onward led the road again
Through the sad uncoloured plain
Under twilight brooding dim,
And along the utmost rim
Wall and rampart risen to sight
Cast a shadow not of night,
And beyond them seemed to glow
Bonfires lighted long ago.
And my dark conductor broke
Silence at my side and spoke,
Saying, 'You conjecture well:
Yonder is the gate of hell.'

Ill as yet the eye could see
The eternal masonry,
But beneath it on the dark
To and fro there stirred a spark.
And again the sombre guide
Knew my question, and replied:
'At hell gate the damned in turn
Pace for sentinel and burn.'

Dully at the leaden sky
Staring, and with idle eye
Measuring the listless plain,
I began to think again.

Many things I thought of then,
Battle, and the loves of men,
Cities entered, oceans crossed,
Knowledge gained and virtue lost,
Cureless folly done and said,
And the lovely way that led
To the slimepit and the mire
And the everlasting fire.
And against a smoulder dun
And a dawn without a sun
Did the nearing bastion loom,
And across the gate of gloom
Still one saw the sentry go,
Trim and burning, to and fro,
One for women to admire
In his finery of fire.
Something, as I watched him pace,
Minded me of time and place,
Soldiers of another corps
And a sentry known before.

Ever darker hell on high
Reared its strength upon the sky,
And our footfall on the track
Fetched the daunting echo back.
But the soldier pacing still
The insuperable sill,
Nursing his tormented pride,
Turned his head to neither side,

Sunk into himself apart
And the hell-fire of his heart.
But against our entering in
From the drawbridge Death and Sin
Rose to render key and sword
To their father and their lord.
And the portress foul to see
Lifted up her eyes on me
Smiling, and I made reply:
'Met again, my lass,' said I.
Then the sentry turned his head,
Looked, and knew me, and was Ned.

Once he looked, and halted straight,
Set his back against the gate,
Caught his musket to his chin,
While the hive of hell within
Sent abroad a seething hum
As of towns whose king is come
Leading conquest home from far
And the captives of his war,
And the car of triumph waits,
And they open wide the gates.
But across the entry barred
Straddled the revolted guard,
Weaponed and accoutred well
From the arsenals of hell;
And beside him, sick and white,
Sin to left and Death to right

Turned a countenance of fear
On the flaming mutineer.
Over us the darkness bowed,
And the anger in the cloud
Clenched the lightning for the stroke;
But the traitor musket spoke.

And the hollowness of hell
Sounded as its master fell,
And the mourning echo rolled
Ruin through his kingdom old.
Tyranny and terror flown
Left a pair of friends alone,
And beneath the nether sky
All that stirred was he and I.

Silent, nothing found to say,
We began the backward way;
And the ebbing lustre died
From the soldier at my side,
As in all his spruce attire
Failed the everlasting fire.
Midmost of the homeward track
Once we listened and looked back;
But the city, dusk and mute,
Slept, and there was no pursuit.

XXXII

When I would muse in boyhood
  The wild green woods among,
And nurse resolves and fancies
  Because the world was young,
It was not foes to conquer,
  Nor sweethearts to be kind,
But it was friends to die for
  That I would seek and find.

I sought them far and found them,
  The sure, the straight, the brave,
The hearts I lost my own to,
  The souls I could not save.
They braced their belts about them,
  They crossed in ships the sea,
They sought and found six feet of ground,
  And there they died for me.

XXXIII

When the eye of day is shut,
   And the stars deny their beams,
And about the forest hut
   Blows the roaring wood of dreams,

From deep clay, from desert rock,
   From the sunk sands of the main,
Come not at my door to knock,
   Hearts that loved me not again.

Sleep, be still, turn to your rest
   In the lands where you are laid;
In far lodgings east and west
   Lie down on the beds you made.

In gross marl, in blowing dust,
   In the drowned ooze of the sea,
Where you would not, lie you must,
   Lie you must, and not with me.

XXXIV

THE FIRST OF MAY

The orchards half the way
   From home to Ludlow fair
Flowered on the first of May
   In Mays when I was there;
And seen from stile or turning
   The plume of smoke would show
Where fires were burning
   That went out long ago.

The plum broke forth in green,
   The pear stood high and snowed,
My friends and I between
   Would take the Ludlow road;
Dressed to the nines and drinking
   And light in heart and limb,
And each chap thinking
   The fair was held for him.

Between the trees in flower
   New friends at fairtime tread
The way where Ludlow tower
   Stands planted on the dead.
Our thoughts, a long while after,
   They think, our words they say;
Theirs now's the laughter,
   The fair, the first of May.

Ay, yonder lads are yet
　　The fools that we were then;
For oh, the sons we get
　　Are still the sons of men.
The sumless tale of sorrow
　　Is all unrolled in vain:
May comes to-morrow
　　And Ludlow fair again.

XXXV

When first my way to fair I took
    Few pence in purse had I,
And long I used to stand and look
    At things I could not buy.

Now times are altered: if I care
    To buy a thing, I can;
The pence are here and here's the fair,
    But where's the lost young man?

— To think that two and two are four
    And neither five nor three
The heart of man has long been sore
    And long 'tis like to be.

XXXVI

REVOLUTION

West and away the wheels of darkness roll,
　Day's beamy banner up the east is borne,
Spectres and fears, the nightmare and her foal,
　Drown in the golden deluge of the morn.

But over sea and continent from sight
　Safe to the Indies has the earth conveyed
The vast and moon-eclipsing cone of night,
　Her towering foolscap of eternal shade.

See, in mid heaven the sun is mounted; hark,
　The belfries tingle to the noonday chime.
'Tis silent, and the subterranean dark
　Has crossed the nadir, and begins to climb.

Last Poems

EPITAPH ON AN ARMY OF MERCENARIES

These, in the day when heaven was falling,
  The hour when earth's foundations fled,
Followed their mercenary calling
  And took their wages and are dead.

Their shoulders held the sky suspended;
  They stood, and earth's foundations stay;
What God abandoned, these defended,
  And saved the sum of things for pay.

XXXVIII

Oh stay at home, my lad, and plough
   The land and not the sea,
And leave the soldiers at their drill,
And all about the idle hill
   Shepherd your sheep with me.

Oh stay with company and mirth
   And daylight and the air;
Too full already is the grave
Of fellows that were good and brave
   And died because they were.

XXXIX

When summer's end is nighing
  And skies at evening cloud,
I muse on change and fortune
  And all the feats I vowed
  When I was young and proud.

The weathercock at sunset
  Would lose the slanted ray,
And I would climb the beacon
  That looked to Wales away
  And saw the last of day.

From hill and cloud and heaven
  The hues of evening died;
Night welled through lane and hollow
  And hushed the countryside,
  But I had youth and pride.

And I with earth and nightfall
  In converse high would stand,
Late, till the west was ashen
  And darkness hard at hand,
  And the eye lost the land.

The year might age, and cloudy
  The lessening day might close,
But air of other summers
  Breathed from beyond the snows,
  And I had hope of those.

Last Poems

They came and were and are not
And come no more anew;
And all the years and seasons
That ever can ensue
Must now be worse and few.

So here's an end of roaming
On eves when autumn nighs:
The ear too fondly listens
For summer's parting sighs,
And then the heart replies.

147

X L

Tell me not here, it needs not saying,
   What tune the enchantress plays
In aftermaths of soft September
   Or under blanching mays,
For she and I were long acquainted
   And I knew all her ways.

On russet floors, by waters idle,
   The pine lets fall its cone;
The cuckoo shouts all day at nothing
   In leafy dells alone;
And traveller's joy beguiles in autumn
   Hearts that have lost their own.

On acres of the seeded grasses
   The changing burnish heaves;
Or marshalled under moons of harvest
   Stand still all night the sheaves;
Or beeches strip in storms for winter
   And stain the wind with leaves.

Possess, as I possessed a season,
   The countries I resign,
Where over elmy plains the highway
   Would mount the hills and shine,
And full of shade the pillared forest
   Would murmur and be mine.

For nature, heartless, witless nature,
    Will neither care nor know
What stranger's feet may find the meadow
    And trespass there and go,
Nor ask amid the dews of morning
    If they are mine or no.

XLI

FANCY'S KNELL

When lads were home from labour
   At Abdon under Clee,
A man would call his neighbour
   And both would send for me.
And where the light in lances
   Across the mead was laid,
There to the dances
   I fetched my flute and played.

Ours were idle pleasures,
   Yet oh, content we were,
The young to wind the measures,
   The old to heed the air;
And I to lift with playing
   From tree and tower and steep
The light delaying,
   And flute the sun to sleep.

The youth toward his fancy
   Would turn his brow of tan,
And Tom would pair with Nancy
   And Dick step off with Fan;
The girl would lift her glances
   To his, and both be mute:
Well went the dances
   At evening to the flute.

Wenlock Edge was umbered,
   And bright was Abdon Burf,
And warm between them slumbered
   The smooth green miles of turf;
Until from grass and clover
   The upshot beam would fade,
And England over
   Advanced the lofty shade.

The lofty shade advances,
   I fetch my flute and play:
Come, lads, and learn the dances
   And praise the tune to-day.
To-morrow, more's the pity,
   Away we both must hie,
To air the ditty,
   And to earth I.

MORE POEMS

They say my verse is sad: no wonder;
  Its narrow measure spans
Tears of eternity, and sorrow,
  Not mine, but man's.

This is for all ill-treated fellows
  Unborn and unbegot,
For them to read when they're in trouble
  And I am not.

More Poems

I

EASTER HYMN

If in that Syrian garden, ages slain,
You sleep, and know not you are dead in vain,
Nor even in dreams behold how dark and bright
Ascends in smoke and fire by day and night
The hate you died to quench and could but fan,
Sleep well and see no morning, son of man.

But if, the grave rent and the stone rolled by,
At the right hand of majesty on high
You sit, and sitting so remember yet
Your tears, your agony and bloody sweat,
Your cross and passion and the life you gave,
Bow hither out of heaven and see and save.

II

When Israel out of Egypt came
    Safe in the sea they trod;
By day in cloud, by night in flame,
    Went on before them God.

He brought them with a stretched out hand
    Dry-footed through the foam,
Past sword and famine, rock and sand,
    Lust and rebellion, home.

I never over Horeb heard
    The blast of advent blow;
No fire-faced prophet brought me word
    Which way behoved me go.

Ascended is the cloudy flame,
    The mount of thunder dumb;
The tokens that to Israel came,
    To me they have not come.

I see the country far away
    Where I shall never stand;
The heart goes where no footstep may
    Into the promised land.

The realm I look upon and die
    Another man will own;
He shall attain the heaven that I
    Perish and have not known.

But I will go where they are hid
    That never were begot,
To my inheritance amid
    The nation that is not.

III

For these of old the trader
   Unpearled the Indian seas,
The nations of the nadir
   Were diamondless for these;

A people prone and haggard
   Beheld their lightnings hurled:
All round, like Sinai, staggered
   The sceptre-shaken world.

But now their coins are tarnished,
   Their towers decayed away,
Their kingdom swept and garnished
   For haler kings than they;

Their arms the rust hath eaten,
   Their statutes none regard:
Arabia shall not sweeten
   Their dust, with all her nard.

They cease from long vexation,
   Their nights, their days are done,
The pale, the perished nation
   That never see the sun;

From the old deep-dusted annals
   The years erase their tale,
And round them race the channels
   That take no second sail.

More Poems

IV

THE SAGE TO THE YOUNG MAN

O youth whose heart is right,
   Whose loins are girt to gain
The hell-defended height
   Where Virtue beckons plain;

Who seest the stark array
   And hast not stayed to count
But singly wilt assay
   The many-cannoned mount:

Well is thy war begun;
   Endure, be strong and strive;
But think not, O my son,
   To save thy soul alive.

Wilt thou be true and just
   And clean and kind and brave?
Well; but for all thou dost,
   Be sure it shall not save.

Thou, when the night falls deep,
   Thou, though the mount be won,
High heart, thou shalt but sleep
   The sleep denied to none.

Others, or ever thou,
   To scale those heights were sworn;
And some achieved, but now
   They never see the morn.

How shouldst thou keep the prize?
   Thou wast not born for aye.
Content thee if thine eyes
   Behold it in thy day.

O youth that wilt attain,
   On, for thine hour is short.
It may be thou shalt gain
   The hell-defended fort.

More Poems

V

The snows are fled away, leaves on the shaws
  And grasses in the mead renew their birth,
The river to the river-bed withdraws,
  And altered is the fashion of the earth.

The Nymphs and Graces three put off their fear
  And unapparelled in the woodland play.
The swift hour and the brief prime of the year
  Say to the soul, *Thou wast not born for aye.*

Thaw follows frost; hard on the heel of spring
  Treads summer sure to die, for hard on hers
Comes autumn, with his apples scattering;
  Then back to wintertide, when nothing stirs.

But oh, whate'er the sky-led seasons mar,
  Moon upon moon rebuilds it with her beams:
Come *we* where Tullus and where Ancus are,
  And good Aeneas, we are dust and dreams.

Torquatus, if the gods in heaven shall add
  The morrow to the day, what tongue has told?
Feast then thy heart, for what thy heart has had
  The fingers of no heir will ever hold.

When thou descendest once the shades among,
    The stern assize and equal judgment o'er,
Not thy long lineage nor thy golden tongue,
    No, nor thy righteousness, shall friend thee more.

Night holds Hippolytus the pure of stain,
    Diana steads him nothing, he must stay;
And Theseus leaves Pirithöus in the chain
    The love of comrades cannot take away.

V I

I to my perils
   Of cheat and charmer
   Came clad in armour
    By stars benign.
Hope lies to mortals
   And most believe her,
   But man's deceiver
    Was never mine.

The thoughts of others
   Were light and fleeting,
   Of lovers' meeting
    Or luck or fame.
Mine were of trouble,
   And mine were steady,
   So I was ready
    When trouble came.

VII

Stars, I have seen them fall,
  But when they drop and die
No star is lost at all
  From all the star-sown sky.
The toil of all that be
  Helps not the primal fault;
It rains into the sea,
  And still the sea is salt.

VIII

Give me a land of boughs in leaf,
  A land of trees that stand;
Where trees are fallen, there is grief;
  I love no leafless land.

Alas, the country whence I fare,
  It is where I would stay;
And where I would not, it is there
  That I shall be for aye.

And one remembers and forgets,
  But 'tis not found again,
Not though they hale in crimsoned nets
  The sunset from the main.

I X

When green buds hang in the elm like dust
  And sprinkle the lime like rain,
Forth I wander, forth I must,
  And drink of life again.

Forth I must by hedgerow bowers
  To look at the leaves uncurled,
And stand in fields where cuckoo flowers
  Are lying about the world.

X

The weeping Pleiads wester,
    And the moon is under seas;
From bourn to bourn of midnight
    Far sighs the rainy breeze:

It sighs from a lost country
    To a land I have not known;
The weeping Pleiads wester,
    And I lie down alone.

XI

The rainy Pleiads wester,
  Orion plunges prone,
The stroke of midnight ceases
  And I lie down alone.

The rainy Pleiads wester
  And seek beyond the sea
The head that I shall dream of
  That will not dream of me.

XII

I promise nothing: friends will part;
  All things may end, for all began;
And truth and singleness of heart
  Are mortal even as is man.

But this unlucky love should last
  When answered passions thin to air;
Eternal fate so deep has cast
  Its sure foundation of despair.

XIII

I lay me down and slumber
   And every morn revive.
Whose is the night-long breathing
   That keeps me man alive?

When I was off to dreamland
   And left my limbs forgot,
Who stayed at home to mind them,
   And breathed when I did not?

   .   .   .   .   .

— I waste my time in talking,
   No heed at all takes he,
My kind and foolish comrade
   That breathes all night for me.

XIV

The farms of home lie lost in even,
  I see far off the steeple stand;
West and away from here to heaven
  Still is the land.

There if I go no girl will greet me,
  No comrade hollo from the hill,
No dog run down the yard to meet me:
  The land is still.

The land is still by farm and steeple,
  And still for me the land may stay:
There I was friends with perished people,
  And there lie they.

X V

Tarry, delight, so seldom met,
    So sure to perish, tarry still;
Forbear to cease or languish yet,
    Though soon you must and will.

By Sestos town, in Hero's tower,
    On Hero's heart Leander lies;
The signal torch has burned its hour
    And sputters as it dies.

Beneath him, in the nighted firth,
    Between two continents complain
The seas he swam from earth to earth
    And he must swim again.

XVI

How clear, how lovely bright,
How beautiful to sight
    Those beams of morning play;
How heaven laughs out with glee
Where, like a bird set free,
Up from the eastern sea
    Soars the delightful day.

To-day I shall be strong,
No more shall yield to wrong,
    Shall squander life no more;
Days lost, I know not how,
I shall retrieve them now;
Now I shall keep the vow
    I never kept before.

Ensanguining the skies
How heavily it dies
    Into the west away;
Past touch and sight and sound
Not further to be found
How hopeless underground
    Falls the remorseful day.

XVII

Bells in tower at evening toll,
And the day forsakes the soul;
Soon will evening's self be gone
And the whispering night come on.

Blame not thou the blinded light
Nor the whisper of the night:
Though the whispering night were still,
Yet the heart would counsel ill.

XVIII

Delight it is in youth and May
  To see the morn arise,
And more delight to look all day
  A lover in the eyes.
Oh maiden, let your distaff be,
And pace the flowery meads with me,
  And I will tell you lies.

'Tis blithe to see the sunshine fail,
  And hear the land grow still,
And listen till the nightingale
  Is heard beneath the hill.
Oh follow me where she is flown
Into the leafy woods alone,
  And I will work you ill.

XIX

The mill-stream, now that noises cease,
Is all that does not hold its peace;
Under the bridge it murmurs by,
And here are night and hell and I.

Who made the world I cannot tell;
'Tis made, and here am I in hell.
My hand, though now my knuckles bleed,
I never soiled with such a deed.

And so, no doubt, in time gone by,
Some have suffered more than I,
Who only spend the night alone
And strike my fist upon the stone.

XX

Like mine, the veins of these that slumber
   Leapt once with dancing fires divine;
The blood of all this noteless number
   Ran red like mine.

How still, with every pulse in station,
   Frost in the founts that used to leap,
The put-to-death, the perished nation
   How sound they sleep!

These too, these veins which life convulses,
   Wait but a while, shall cease to bound;
I with the ice in all my pulses
   Shall sleep as sound.

XXI

The world goes none the lamer,
  For ought that I can see,
Because this cursed trouble
  Has struck my days and me.

The stars of heaven are steady,
  The founded hills remain,
Though I to earth and darkness
  Return in blood and pain.

Farewell to all belongings
  I won or bought or stole;
Farewell, my lusty carcase,
  Farewell, my aery soul.

Oh worse remains for others,
  And worse to fear had I
Than here at four-and-twenty
  To lay me down and die.

XXII

Ho, everyone that thirsteth
   And hath the price to give,
Come to the stolen waters,
   Drink and your soul shall live

Come to the stolen waters,
   And leap the guarded pale,
And pull the flower in season
   Before desire shall fail.

It shall not last for ever,
   No more than earth and skies;
But he that drinks in season
   Shall live before he dies.

June suns, you cannot store them
   To warm the winter's cold,
The lad that hopes for heaven
   Shall fill his mouth with mould.

XXIII

Crossing alone the nighted ferry
   With the one coin for fee,
Whom, on the wharf of Lethe waiting,
   Count you to find? Not me.

The brisk fond lackey to fetch and carry,
   The true, sick-hearted slave,
Expect him not in the just city
   And free land of the grave.

XXIV

Stone, steel, dominions pass,
    Faith too, no wonder;
So leave alone the grass
    That I am under.

All knots that lovers tie
    Are tied to sever;
Here shall your sweet-heart lie,
    Untrue for ever.

X X V

Yon flakes that fret the eastern sky
   Lead back my day of birth;
The far, wide-wandered hour when I
   Came crying upon earth.

Then came I crying, and to-day,
   With heavier cause to plain,
Depart I into death away,
   Not to be born again.

XXVI

Good creatures, do you love your lives
  And have you ears for sense?
Here is a knife like other knives,
  That cost me eighteen pence.

I need but stick it in my heart
  And down will come the sky,
And earth's foundations will depart
  And all you folk will die.

XXVII

To stand up straight and tread the turning mill,
To lie flat and know nothing and be still,
Are the two trades of man; and which is worse
I know not, but I know that both are ill.

XXVIII

He, standing hushed, a pace or two apart,
  Among the bluebells of the listless plain,
Thinks, and remembers how he cleansed his heart
  And washed his hands in innocence in vain.

XXIX

From the wash the laundress sends
My collars home with ravelled ends;
I must fit, now these are frayed,
My neck with new ones London-made.

Homespun collars, homespun hearts,
Wear to rags in foreign parts.
Mine at least's as good as done,
And I must get a London one.

X X X

Shake hands, we shall never be friends, all's over;
    I only vex you the more I try.
All's wrong that ever I've done or said,
And nought to help it in this dull head:
    Shake hands, here's luck, good-bye.

But if you come to a road where danger
    Or guilt or anguish or shame's to share,
Be good to the lad that loves you true
And the soul that was born to die for you,
    And whistle and I'll be there.

XXXI

Because I liked you better
   Than suits a man to say,
It irked you, and I promised
   To throw the thought away.

To put the world between us
   We parted, stiff and dry;
'Good-bye', said you, 'forget me.'
   'I will, no fear', said I.

If here, where clover whitens
   The dead man's knoll, you pass,
And no tall flower to meet you
   Starts in the trefoiled grass,

Halt by the headstone naming
   The heart no longer stirred,
And say the lad that loved you
   Was one that kept his word.

XXXII

With seed the sowers scatter
　　The furrows as they go;
Poor lads, 'tis little matter
　　How many sorts they sow,
　　For only one will grow.

The charlock on the fallow
　　Will take the traveller's eyes,
And gild the ploughland sallow
　　With flowers before it dies,
　　But twice 'twill not arise.

The stinging nettle only
　　Will still be found to stand:
The numberless, the lonely,
　　The thronger of the land,
　　The leaf that hurts the hand.

It thrives, come sun, come showers,
　　Blow east, blow west, it springs;
It peoples towns, and towers
　　About the courts of Kings,
　　And touch it and it stings.

XXXIII

On forelands high in heaven,
   'Tis many a year gone by,
Amidst the fall of even
   Would stand my friends and I.
Before our foolish faces
   Lay lands we did not see;
Our eyes were in the places
   Where we should never be.

Oh, the pearl seas are yonder,
   The amber-sanded shore;
Shires where the girls are fonder,
   Towns where the pots hold more.
And here fret we and moulder
   By grange and rick and shed
And every moon are older,
   And soon we shall be dead.

Heigho, 'twas true and pity;
   But there we lads must stay.
Troy was a steepled city,
   But Troy was far away.
And round we turned lamenting
   To homes we longed to leave,
And silent hills indenting
   The orange band of eve.

I see the air benighted
  And all the dusking dales,
And lamps in England lighted,
  And evening wrecked in Wales;
And starry darkness paces
  The road from sea to sea,
And blots the foolish faces
  Of my poor friends and me.

XXXIV

Young is the blood that yonder
    Strides out the dusty mile,
And breasts the hillside highway
    And whistles loud the while,
    And vaults the stile.

On miry meads in winter
    The football sprang and fell;
May stuck the land with wickets:
    For all the eye could tell,
    The world went well.

Yet well, God knows, it went not,
    God knows, it went awry;
For me, one flowery Maytime,
    It went so ill that I
    Designed to die.

And if so long I carry
    The lot that season marred,
'Tis that the sons of Adam
    Are not so evil-starred
    As they are hard.

Yet flesh, now too, has thorn-pricks,
    And shoulders carry care,
Even as in other seasons,
    When I and not my heir
    Was young and there.

More Poems

Young is the blood that yonder
    Succeeds to rick and fold,
Fresh are the form and favour
    And new the minted mould:
    The thoughts are old.

XXXV

Half way, for one commandment broken,
  The woman made her endless halt,
And she to-day, a glistering token,
  Stands in the wilderness of salt.
Behind, the vats of judgment brewing
  Thundered, and thick the brimstone snowed;
He to the hill of his undoing
  Pursued his road.

XXXVI

Here dead lie we because we did not choose
   To live and shame the land from which we sprung.
Life, to be sure, is nothing much to lose;
   But young men think it is, and we were young.

XXXVII

I did not lose my heart in summer's even,
  When roses to the moonrise burst apart:
When plumes were under heel and lead was flying,
  In blood and smoke and flame I lost my heart.

I lost it to a soldier and a foeman,
  A chap that did not kill me, but he tried;
That took the sabre straight and took it striking,
  And laughed and kissed his hand to me and died.

XXXVIII

By shores and woods and steeples
   Rejoicing hearts receive
Poured on a hundred peoples
   The far-shed alms of eve.

Her hands are filled with slumber
   For world-wide labourers worn;
Yet those are more in number
   That know her not from morn.

Now who sees night for ever,
   He sees no happier sight:
Night and no moon and never
   A star upon the night.

XXXIX

My dreams are of a field afar
　　And blood and smoke and shot.
There in their graves my comrades are,
　　In my grave I am not.

I too was taught the trade of man
　　And spelt the lesson plain;
But they, when I forgot and ran,
　　Remembered and remain.

X L

Farewell to a name and a number,
  Recalled again
To darkness and silence and slumber
  In blood and pain.

So ceases and turns to the thing
  He was born to be
A soldier cheap to the King
  And dear to me;

So smothers in blood the burning
  And flaming flight
Of valour and truth, returning
  To dust and night.

X L I

He looked at me with eyes I thought
    I was not like to find;
The voice he begged for pence with brought
    Another man to mind.

Oh, no, lad, never touch your cap;
    It is not my half-crown;
You have it from a better chap
    That long ago lay down.

Turn east and over Thames to Kent
    And come to the sea's brim,
And find his everlasting tent
    And touch your cap to him.

XLII

A. J. J.

When he's returned I'll tell him – oh,
    Dear fellow, I forgot:
Time was you would have cared to know,
    But now it matters not.

I mourn you, and you heed not how;
    Unsaid the word must stay;
Last month was time enough, but now
    The news must keep for aye.

Oh, many a month before I learn
    Will find me starting still
And listening, as the days return,
    For him that never will.

Strange, strange to think his blood is cold
    And mine flows easy on;
And that straight look, that heart of gold,
    That grace, that manhood gone.

The word unsaid will stay unsaid
    Though there was much to say;
Last month was time enough: he's dead,
    The news must keep for aye.

XLIII

I wake from dreams and turning
　My vision on the height
I scan the beacons burning
　About the fields of night.

Each in its steadfast station
　In flaming heaven they flare;
They sign with conflagration
　The empty moors of air.

The signal-fires of warning
　They blaze, but none regard;
And on through night to morning
　The world runs ruinward.

XLIV

Far known to sea and shore,
  Foursquare and founded well,
A thousand years it bore,
  And then the belfry fell.
    The steersman of Triest
    Looked where his mark should be,
    But empty was the west
    And Venice under sea.

From dusty wreck dispersed
  Its stature mounts amain;
On surer foot than first
  The belfry stands again.
    At to-fall of the day
    Again its curfew tolls
    And burdens far away
    The green and sanguine shoals.

It looks to north and south,
  It looks to east and west;
It guides to Lido mouth
  The steersman of Triest.
    Andrea, fare you well;
    Venice, farewell to thee.
    The tower that stood and fell
    Is not rebuilt in me.

X L V

Smooth between sea and land
Is laid the yellow sand,
And here through summer days
The seed of Adam plays.

Here the child comes to found
His unremaining mound,
And the grown lad to score
Two names upon the shore.

Here, on the level sand,
Between the sea and land,
What shall I build or write
Against the fall of night?

Tell me of runes to grave
That hold the bursting wave,
Or bastions to design
For longer date than mine.

Shall it be Troy or Rome
I fence against the foam,
Or my own name, to stay
When I depart for aye?

Nothing: too near at hand,
Planing the figured sand,
Effacing clean and fast
Cities not built to last
And charms devised in vain,
Pours the confounding main.

XLVI

THE LAND OF BISCAY

Sons of landsmen, sons of seamen,
    hear the tale of grief and me,
Looking from the land of Biscay
    on the waters of the sea.

Looking from the land of Biscay
    over Ocean to the sky
On the far-beholding foreland
    paced at even grief and I.
There, as warm the west was burning
    and the east uncoloured cold,
Down the waterway of sunset
    drove to shore a ship of gold.
Gold of mast and gold of cordage,
    gold of sail to sight was she,
And she glassed her ensign golden
    in the waters of the sea.

Oh, said I, my friend and lover,
    take we now that ship and sail
Outward in the ebb of hues and
    steer upon the sunset trail;
Leave the night to fall behind us
    and the clouding counties leave:
Help for you and me is yonder,
    in the havens west of eve.

Under hill she neared the landing,
    till the gazer could behold
On the golden deck the steersman
    standing at the helm of gold,
Man and ship and sky and water
    burning in a single flame;
And the mariner of Ocean
    he was calling as he came:
From the highway of the sunset
    he was shouting on the sea,
'Landsman of the land of Biscay,
    have you help for grief and me?'

When I heard I did not answer,
    I stood mute and shook my head:
Son of earth and son of Ocean,
    much we thought and nothing said.
Grief and I abode the nightfall,
    to the sunset grief and he
Turned them from the land of Biscay
    on the waters of the sea.

XLVII

FOR MY FUNERAL

O thou that from thy mansion
   Through time and place to roam,
Dost send abroad thy children,
   And then dost call them home,

That men and tribes and nations
   And all thy hand hath made
May shelter them from sunshine
   In thine eternal shade:

We now to peace and darkness
   And earth and thee restore
Thy creature that thou madest
   And wilt cast forth no more.

XLVIII

PARTA QUIES

Good-night; ensured release,
Imperishable peace,
    Have these for yours,
While sea abides, and land,
And earth's foundations stand,
    And heaven endures.

When earth's foundations flee,
Nor sky nor land nor sea
    At all is found,
Content you, let them burn:
It is not your concern;
    Sleep on, sleep sound.

ADDITIONAL POEMS

I

ATYS

'Lydians, lords of Hermus river,
    Sifters of the golden loam,
See you yet the lances quiver
    And the hunt returning home?'

'King, the star that shuts the even
    Calls the sheep from Tmolus down;
Home return the doves from heaven,
    And the prince to Sardis town.'

From the hunting heavy laden
    Up the Mysian road they ride;
And the star that mates the maiden
    Leads his son to Croesus' side.

'Lydians, under stream and fountain
    Finders of the golden vein,
Riding from Olympus mountain,
    Lydians, see you Atys plain?'

'King, I see the Phrygian stranger
    And the guards in hunter's trim,
Saviours of thy son from danger;
    Them I see. I see not him.'

'Lydians, as the troop advances,
    – It is eve and I am old –
Tell me why they trail their lances,
    Washers of the sands of gold.

'I am old and day is ending
    And the wildering night comes on;
Up the Mysian entry wending,
    Lydians, Lydians, what is yon?'

Hounds behind their master whining,
    Huntsmen pacing dumb beside,
On his breast the boar-spear shining,
    Home they bear his father's pride.

II

Oh were he and I together,
   Shipmates on the fleeted main,
Sailing through the summer weather
   To the spoil of France or Spain.

Oh were he and I together,
   Locking hands and taking leave,
Low upon the trampled heather
   In the battle lost at eve.

Now are he and I asunder
   And asunder to remain;
Kingdoms are for others' plunder,
   And content for other slain.

III

When Adam walked in Eden young,
  Happy, 'tis writ, was he,
While high the fruit of knowledge hung
  Unbitten on the tree.

Happy was he the livelong day;
  I doubt 'tis written wrong:
The heart of man, for all they say,
  Was never happy long.

And now my feet are tired of rest,
  And here they will not stay,
And the soul fevers in my breast
  And aches to be away.

I V

It is no gift I tender,
    A loan is all I can;
But do not scorn the lender;
    Man gets no more from man.

Oh, mortal man may borrow
    What mortal man can lend;
And 'twill not end to-morrow,
    Though sure enough 'twill end.

If death and time are stronger,
    A love may yet be strong;
The world will last for longer,
    But this will last for long.

Additional Poems

V

Here are the skies, the planets seven,
And all the starry train;
Content you with the mimic heaven,
And on the earth remain.[1]

Written by A. E. H. on the flyleaf of a copy of *Manilius*,
Book I, which he gave to Walter Headlam.

V I

Ask me no more, for fear I should reply;
   Others have held their tongues, and so can I;
Hundreds have died, and told no tale before:
   Ask me no more, for fear I should reply —

How one was true and one was clean of stain
   And one was braver than the heavens are high,
And one was fond of me: and all are slain.
   Ask me no more, for fear I should reply.

VII

He would not stay for me; and who can wonder?
He would not stay for me to stand and gaze.
I shook his hand and tore my heart in sunder
And went with half my life about my ways.

Additional Poems

VIII

Now to her lap the incestuous earth
　　The son she bore has ta'en.
And other sons she brings to birth
　　But not my friend again.

Additional Poems

When the bells justle in the tower
  The hollow night amid,
Then on my tongue the taste is sour
  Of all I ever did.

X

Oh, on my breast in days hereafter
    Light the earth should lie,
Such weight to bear is now the air,
    So heavy hangs the sky.

X I

GOD'S ACRE

Morning up the eastern stair
Marches, azuring the air,
And the foot of twilight still
Is stolen toward the western sill.
Blithe the maids to milking, blithe
Men in hayfields stone the scythe;
All the land's alive around
Except the churchyard's idle ground.
There's empty acres west and east,
But 'tis from God's we gather least,
This hopeless garden that they sow
With the seeds that never grow.
They shall have breath that never were,
But he that was shall have it ne'er;
The unconceived and unbegot
Shall look on heaven, but he shall not.
The heart with many wild fires lit,
Ice is not so cold as it.
The thirst that rivers could not lay
A little dust has quenched for aye;
And in a fathom's compass lie
Thoughts much wider than the sky.

XII

AN EPITAPH

Stay, if you list, O passer by the way;
Yet night approaches; better not to stay.
 I never sigh, nor flush, nor knit the brow,
 Nor grieve to think how ill God made me, now.
Here, with one balm for many fevers found,
Whole of an ancient evil, I sleep sound.

XIII

Oh turn not in from marching
    To taverns on the way.
The drought and thirst and parching
    A little dust will lay,
    And take desire away.

Oh waste no words a-wooing
    The soft sleep to your bed;
She is not worth pursuing,
    You will so soon be dead;
    And death will serve instead.

XIV

'Oh is it the jar of nations,
   The noise of a world run mad,
The fleeing of earth's foundations?'
   Yes, yes; lie quiet, my lad.

'Oh is it my country calling?
   And whom will my country find
To shore up the sky from falling?'
   My business; never you mind.

'Oh is it the newsboys crying
   Lost battle, retreat, despair,
And honour and England dying?'
   Well, fighting-cock, what if it were?

The devil this side of the darnels
   Is having a dance with man,
And quarrelsome chaps in charnels
   Must bear it as best they can.

X V

'Tis five years since, 'An end', said I;
'I'll march no further, time to die.
All's lost; no worse has heaven to give.'
Worse it has given, and yet I live.

I shall not die to-day, no fear;
I shall live yet for many a year,
And see worse ills and worse again,
And die of age and not of pain.

When God would rear from earth aloof
The blue height of the hollow roof,
He sought him pillars sure and strong,
And ere he found them sought them long.

The stark steel splintered from the thrust,
The basalt mountain sprang to dust,
The blazing pier of diamond flawed
In shards of rainbows all abroad.

What found he, that the heavens stand fast?
What pillar proven firm at last
Bears up so light that world-seen span?
The heart of man, the heart of man.

XVI

Some can gaze and not be sick,
But I could never learn the trick.
There's this to say for blood and breath,
They give a man a taste for death.

XVII

The stars have not dealt me the worst they could do:
My pleasures are plenty, my troubles are two.
But oh, my two troubles they reave me of rest,
The brains in my head and the heart in my breast.

Oh grant me the ease that is granted so free,
The birthright of multitudes, give it to me,
That relish their victuals and rest on their bed
With flint in the bosom and guts in the head.

XVIII

Oh who is that young sinner with the handcuffs on his
    wrists?
And what has he been after that they groan and shake
    their fists?
And wherefore is he wearing such a conscience-stricken
    air?
Oh they're taking him to prison for the colour of his hair.

'Tis a shame to human nature, such a head of hair as his;
In the good old time 'twas hanging for the colour that it is;
Though hanging isn't bad enough and flaying would be
    fair
For the nameless and abominable colour of his hair.

Oh a deal of pains he's taken and a pretty price he's paid
To hide his poll or dye it of a mentionable shade;
But they've pulled the beggar's hat off for the world to
    see and stare,
And they're taking him to justice for the colour of his hair.

Now 'tis oakum for his fingers and the treadmill for his
    feet,
And the quarry-gang on Portland in the cold and in the
    heat,
And between his spells of labour in the time he has to
    spare
He can curse the God that made him for the colour of his
    hair.

XIX

THE DEFEATED

In battles of no renown
My fellows and I fell down,
And over the dead men roar
The battles they lost before.

The thunderstruck flagstaffs fall,
The earthquake breaches the wall,
The far-felled steeples resound,
And we lie under the ground.

O soldiers, saluted afar
By them that had seen your star,
In conquest and freedom and pride
Remember your friends that died.

Amid rejoicing and song
Remember, my lads, how long,
How deep the innocent trod
The grapes of the anger of God.

XX

I shall not die for you,
    Another fellow may;
Good lads are left and true
    Though one departs away.
    But he departs to-day
And leaves his work to do,
    For I was luckless aye
And shall not die for you.

XXI

NEW YEAR'S EVE

The end of the year fell chilly
   Between a moon and a moon;
Thorough the twilight shrilly
   The bells rang, ringing no tune.

The windows stained with story,
   The walls with miracle scored,
Were hidden for gloom and glory
   Filling the house of the Lord.

Arch and aisle and rafter
   And roof-tree dizzily high
Were full of weeping and laughter
   And song and saying good-bye.

There stood in the holy places
   A multitude none could name,
Ranks of dreadful faces,
   Flaming, transfigured in flame.

Crown and tiar and mitre
   Were starry with gold and gem;
Christmas never was whiter
   Than fear on the face of them.

In aisles that emperors vaulted
   For a faith the world confessed,
Abasing the Host exalted,
   They worshipped towards the west.

They brought with laughter oblation;
    They prayed, not bowing the head;
They made without tear lamentation,
    And rendered me answer and said:

'Oh thou that seest our sorrow,
    It fares with us even thus:
To-day we are gods, to-morrow
    Hell have mercy on us.

'Lo, morning over our border
    From out of the west comes cold;
Down ruins the ancient order
    And empire builded of old.

'Our house at even is queenly
    With psalm and censers alight:
Look thou never so keenly
    Thou shalt not find us to-night.

'We are come to the end appointed
    With sands not many to run;
Divinities disanointed
    And kings whose kingdom is done.

'The peoples knelt down at our portal,
    All kindreds under the sky;
We were gods and implored and immortal
    Then; and to-day we die.'

They turned them again to their praying,
  They worshipped and took no rest,
Singing old tunes and saying
  'We have seen his star in the west',

Old tunes of the sacred psalters,
  Set to wild farewells;
And I left them there at their altars
  Ringing their own dead knells.

XXII

R. L. S.

Home is the sailor, home from sea:
    Her far-borne canvas furled
The ship pours shining on the quay
    The plunder of the world.

Home is the hunter from the hill:
    Fast in the boundless snare
All flesh lies taken at his will
    And every fowl of air.

'Tis evening on the moorland free,
    The starlit wave is still:
Home is the sailor from the sea,
    The hunter from the hill.

XXIII

THE OLIVE

The olive in its orchard
   Should now be rooted sure,
To cast abroad its branches
   And flourish and endure.

Aloft amid the trenches
   Its dressers dug and died;
The olive in its orchard
   Should prosper and abide.

Close should the fruit be clustered
   And light the leaf should wave,
So deep the root is planted
   In the corrupting grave.

TRANSLATIONS

Translations

Aeschylus, *Septem Contra Thebas* (lines 848-860)

Now do our eyes behold
The tidings which were told:
Twin fallen kings, twin perished hopes to mourn,
The slayer, the slain,
The entangled doom forlorn
And ruinous end of twain.
Say, is not sorrow, is not sorrow's sum
On home and hearthstone come?
O waft with sighs the sail from shore,
O smite the bosom, cadencing the oar
That rows beyond the rueful stream for aye
To the far strand,
The ship of souls, the dark,
The unreturning bark
Whereon light never falls nor foot of Day,
Ev'n to the bourne of all, to the unbeholden land.

Translations

Sophocles, *Oedipus Coloneus* (lines 1211-1248)

What man is he that yearneth
    For length unmeasured of days?
Folly mine eye discerneth
    Encompassing all his ways.
For years over-running the measure
    Shall change thee in evil wise:
Grief draweth nigh thee; and pleasure,
    Behold, it is hid from thine eyes.
    This to their wage have they
    Which overlive their day.
And He that looseth from labour
    Doth one with other befriend,
    Whom bride nor bridesmen attend,
Song, nor sound of the tabor,
    Death, that maketh an end.

Thy portion esteem I highest,
    Who wast not ever begot;
Thine next, being born who diest
    And straightway again art not.
With follies light as the feather
    Doth Youth to man befall;
Then evils gather together,
    There wants not one of them all –
    Wrath, envy, discord, strife,
    The sword that seeketh life.

And sealing the sum of trouble
   Doth tottering Age draw nigh,
   Whom friends and kinsfolk fly,
Age, upon whom redouble
   All sorrows under the sky.

This man, as me, even so,
Have the evil days overtaken;
And like as a cape sea-shaken
With tempest at earth's last verges
And shock of all winds that blow,
His head the seas of woe,
The thunders of awful surges
Ruining overflow;
Blown from the fall of even,
   Blown from the dayspring forth,
Blown from the noon in heaven,
   Blown from night and the North.

Translations

Euripides, *Alcestis* (lines 962-1005)

In heaven-high musings and many,
    Far-seeking and deep debate,
Of strong things find I not any
    That is as the strength of Fate.
Help nor healing is told
In soothsayings uttered of old,
In the Thracian runes, the verses
    Engraven of Orpheus' pen;
No balm of virtue to save
Apollo aforetime gave,
Who stayeth with tender mercies
    The plagues of the children of men.

She hath not her habitation
    In temples that hands have wrought;
Him that bringeth oblation,
    Behold, she heedeth him naught.
Be thou not wroth with us more,
O mistress, than heretofore;
For what God willeth soever,
    That thou bringest to be;
Thou breakest in sunder the brand
Far forged in the Iron Land;
Thine heart is cruel, and never
    Came pity anigh unto thee.

Thee too, O King, hath she taken
    And bound in her tenfold chain;
    Yet faint not, neither complain:
The dead thou wilt not awaken
    For all thy weeping again.
They perish, whom gods begot;
The night releaseth them not.
Beloved was she that died
And dear shall ever abide,
For this was the queen among women, Admetus, that lay
    by thy side.

Not as the multitude lowly,
    Asleep in their sepulchres,
    Not as their grave be hers,
But like as the gods held holy,
    The worship of wayfarers.
Yea, all that travel the way
Far off shall see it and say,
Lo, erst for her lord she died,
To-day she sitteth enskied;
Hail, lady, be gracious to usward; that alway her honour
    abide.

NOTE ON THE TEXT

A SHROPSHIRE LAD
The text is based on a collation of the early editions, with occasional reference to Housman's own copy of the second edition (1898) in which he had made a number of corrections. The result was then checked by the errata to the 1927 edition, the latest which Housman is certainly known to have scrutinized for errors. The only changes in wording made by the author since the original printing of 1896 were introduced in 1922. They are 'Loose on the wind' for 'Thick on the wind' at XXXVIII, 10, and 'no more remembered' for 'long since forgotten' at LII, 9.

LAST POEMS
In the preface to this volume, Housman wrote: 'it is best that what I have written should be printed while I am here to see it through the press and control its spelling and punctuation.' Against the last word he pencilled in his own copy: 'Vain hope!' and a direction to p. 52, where he added two punctuation marks which had dropped out between the passing of final proofs and going to press. These corrections were incorporated in the second impression; and since it is confidently believed that no further changes were ever made by the author, this remains the definitive text.

MORE POEMS
The poems in this volume were printed partly from drafts in the author's notebooks, partly from fair copies. In some places among the former (which are in the majority) further scrutiny of the manuscripts has made it possible to present a more correct text. Most of the few changes are matters of punctuation or of a single mistranscribed word, but one or two require a note of explanation.
In II, for instance, it will have been observed that the final stanza, as printed in *More Poems*, has been removed. Closer examination made it clear that this stanza, which reads

> When mixed with me the sandstorms drift
> And nerve and heart and brain
> Are ashes for the air to lift
> And lightly shower again.

does not belong to this poem.
In XIII the manuscript shows that two projected stanzas, between 2 and 3, were to have contained that conversation between the poet and his 'kind and foolish comrade' to which the final stanza refers. The first of these never progressed beyond the last line

> For oh, 'twas never I.

but the second was nearly completed, as follows:

> 'If I were you, young fellow,
> I'd save what breath I had
> And [keep?] the night for sleeping.
> Oh, spare your pains, my lad.'

It seems probable, therefore, that the poem is incomplete; but it has been thought best to preserve it, with this explanation.

Note on the Text

The text of v (*Diffugere Nives*) has been accommodated to that of the original printing in *The Quarto*, 1897 (Vol. III, p. 95); and in XLVIII the original text and the title (from Virgil, *Aeneid*, III, 495) have been restored from the 1881 printing in *Waifs and Strays* (Vol. II, No. VI, Oxford, Blackwell).

ADDITIONAL POEMS
The first eighteen of these, which were printed in Mr. Laurence Housman's *A.E.H., A Memoir*, are in the same case as *More Poems* and have been similarly treated. Of the remaining five the first two are here printed, for the first time in book form, from the manuscripts. The others have been collected from the periodicals in which they originally appeared. *New Year's Eve* dates from 1881 (in *Waifs and Strays*, Vol. III, No. VIII); *R.L.S.* from 1894 (in *The Academy*); *The Olive* from 1902 (*The Outlook*, June 2).

TRANSLATIONS
The three translations from the Greek were published in *Odes from the Greek Dramatists*, edited by A. W. Pollard (London, David Stott, 1890).

INDEX OF FIRST LINES

Index of First Lines

Index of First Lines

Index of First Lines

Index of First Lines

Index of First Lines

INDEX OF TITLED POEMS